The Good News Reader

Reader

Five Short Works

I0141522

Larry L. Armstrong

FaithProbe

ISBN: 0-9823466-3-8
ISBN-13: 978-0-9823466-3-1

DEDICATION

This collection of shorter books is gathered
in honor of the people of
the First Presbyterian Church of Jeannette, PA

Ministry among you was always delightful

CONTENTS

INTRODUCTION TO THE FIVE BOOKS

My desire in bringing these five short works together was to offer a person who is new to the principles of Christian discipleship help in learning how and why believers do what they do. A young disciple (in practice not in age) needs guidance in following Jesus Christ. These short works present various aspects of the basics of Christian life. Follow the principles laid out in them, and you'll become a productive disciple.

GraceTouch: Six Experiences of God's Grace lays a foundation for understanding Christian growth. We live by the touches of divine grace in our lives. Not all possible experiences of grace are mapped out, but six of the most essential are presented.

In *The Flawless Word*, I outline the nature of scripture and its importance for your day-to-day walk with the Lord. Through the use of God's word, we plant our feet on firm ground in this world and learn what pleases him. We discover how we should live.

Seven Ways to Get Close to God is a short pamphlet I wrote to help new Christians find a balanced discipline for their spiritual development. Our life is one of relationship with God through Christ and the Holy Spirit. This short work draws you into the core practices behind faithful discipleship.

Centered Living presents a way to align your heart with Jesus Christ's heart. It takes you into the deeper questions of

Christian behavior and how to bring focus to your conduct. Through it, I hope you'll learn to guard your heart well.

A Crown Forever is a series of sermons which are united by the theme of the *crown* in Christian living. They present a glance at the rewards promised to faithful disciples and instruct you in how to seek the rewards properly.

As you move through these short works, my prayer is that God will clarify and expand upon whom he has called you to be, and why.

Larry L. Armstrong

BOOK ONE
GRACETOUCH: SIX EXPERIENCES OF GOD'S GRACE

The Good News Reader

INTRODUCTION

GraceTouch is about the Christian's experience of God's grace, and how to observe the Lord's interaction with you every day. I want to help you understand six varying ways we discover his favor. Although I call each chapter a first or second or third touch, there isn't a sequential order to what's discussed. Which comes first rebirth or repentance? covenant or calling? As a person analyzes the strokes of mercy on the soul, it's impossible to be certain of the order of the touches. I suspect everyone senses each tap on the shoulder in an order unique to individual need or openness to the Holy Spirit. So don't think about the diverse features of grace as a sequence. They're first or fourth in terms of presentation only, not in their importance and in order of experience.

God's finger caresses or his hand chastens Christians in many ways, not only the six presented here. The six aspects covered in *GraceTouch* were selected because they appear to me to be common to all believers, ways each and every disciple encounters the divine in her or his life. Christians may describe rebirth with a different vocabulary, but all believers are made into new people through Jesus Christ. The Lord establishes a covenant with individual disciples and with the collection of followers we label the church. Repentance is another common way we discover grace operating within and among us. Loyal relationships also develop when we're committed to God and one another through the Master's touch. In the same way, no Christian escapes a calling, and all have communion as a recurring contact with grace.

Use these chapters in *GraceTouch* as a springboard for your private meditation on six fundamental aspects of knowing and serving God through Jesus Christ. Pray and think as you read. Perhaps write out your response to each chapter's subject as a way of analyzing your growth in awareness.

I pray that our Lord will embrace you as you study and as your insight expands. May the Spirit enlarge your faith in Jesus Christ.

Larry L. Armstrong

1
A FIRST TOUCH:
REBIRTH

Have you wondered what the difference is between a Christian and a non-Christian? After all, the world has some nice people in it, but not all nice people want anything to do with Jesus. They live decent lives. They're friendly, and you like them. So what's different between them and you, non-Christian and Christian?

Buried in his letter to the Colossians, in a passage that explained the gap between Christian and non-Christian *behavior*, the apostle Paul spoke about what it means to be born anew, to be a Christian. He said, "...you have taken off your old self with its practices and have put on the new self, which is being renewed in knowledge in the image of its Creator" (Col. 3:9*b*-10). This seems clear enough: Born anew in Christ, you're to live in a Christian way. The first touch of God's gracious finger in your life brings about your rebirth. You've taken off an old suit of clothes and put on a new one. Your life has started again. So you act in newer, better ways.

How you behave is supposed to be a hallmark of your character as a Christian. So it seems as if the expected level of conduct is part of the difference between Jesus' disciples and those who choose not to be his followers. A Christian's behavior is supposed to be of a higher quality. As Jesus said in the Sermon on the Mount, "...unless your righteousness surpasses that of the Pharisees and the teachers of the law, you will certainly not enter the kingdom of heaven" (Mt. 5:20).

A friend of mine once told me he'd become a Christian, which he defined as going to church, when he decided it was time to give up his nightly beers and daily cigarettes. He was partly correct. Being a disciple of Jesus holds you accountable for excellence in your activities. He was incorrect in thinking that better behavior would make him a Christian. It's the other way around. Because God's touch results in a rebirth of godliness in your heart, you start working on the construction of a better personality and the acquiring of higher interests. Rebirth results in renovation!

New Clothing

To be born anew in Christ is to be dressed in new clothing. That's how Paul put it. Off with the old muddy clothes! He called the rags we once wore the "old self." Our characteristic behavior before we were believers included things like hateful desires, impurity, selfishness, sexual immorality, and greed. Sounds like the plot of a modern television series, doesn't it? But those are the old clothes a Christian has to remove. Paul explained the new birth in Christ to the Colossian Christians by saying, "...you have taken off your old self with its practices..."

In other words, prior to following Jesus of Nazareth your habits and thought-patterns were conditioned to the typical human standards. If people left you alone, you tried not to be a bother in their lives. Live, and let live! Let's be friendly and tolerant! Let's stay close, but not too intimate! The usual desire of human beings is for peace, safety, and limited companionship. But these are not very high standards, are they? When you began to learn a Christian way of living, greater value was demanded from your behavior.

If you remove dirty slacks and shirt, you need to wear something else. So on with the new! The apostle Paul continued his instruction on the new birth. "You've put on a new self," he told the Colossians. In other words, now you follow Jesus, so wear something better than you used to wear. Throw away the worn-out apparel! Get rid of anger, rage, malice, slander, and filthy language. "Do not lie to each other..." Paul demanded. Notice that two of these bad habits are *internal* sins—rage and malice—and the rest are sins of the lips. They extend *outside* yourself. They smack against other people. Anger leads you to filthy talk, to slander, to lies. These are the clothes you used to wear before you knew Jesus. Put on new garments! Praise others, ask for forgiveness, offer forgiveness.

Do you know how long the proverb, "The clothes make the man," has been around? At least since the time of the Romans. It first appeared in their literature. *The clothes make the man.* There's truth to it. As Thomas Fuller pointed out, "Good clothes open all doors." That's why people advise you to dress well for a job interview. Yet this bothers some people. Henry David Thoreau warned, "Beware of all enterprises that require new clothes!"

You have a different perspective on the world than a non-Christian has. This is what Paul was driving at when he wrote:

> Since "...you have been raised with Christ, set your hearts on things above, where Christ is seated at the right hand of God. Set your minds on things above, not on earthly things. For you died, and your life is now hidden with Christ in God. When Christ, who is your life, appears, then you also will appear with him in glory" (Col. 3:1-4).

Born anew in Christ, you focus your attention on the concerns of heaven, and you occupy yourself with the business of the Father's heavenly kingdom. The finger of grace has tapped your shoulder. It's as if you died and now live a new life. Behave like it!

New Character

To be born anew in Christ is to be renewed in character. You once conducted yourself in the same unthinking, self-centered, godless way worldly-minded people believe they're free to choose. Paul explained, "You used to walk in these ways, in the life you once lived. But now you must rid yourselves of all such things as these: anger, rage, malice, slander, and filthy language from your lips" (Col. 3:7-8). The apostle mentioned prejudicial hatred between "Greek or Jew, circumcised or uncircumcised, barbarian, Scythian, slave or free." Instead, you and I are to focus on Jesus Christ. We're called to be reborn in his image. He alone is all in all.

This means you have to be renewed in your intellect, your ability to think, reason and select between options with wisdom. As Paul said to the Colossians about the effect of their new birth, "You've put on a new self, which is being renewed in knowledge." What sort of knowledge? The knowledge that God rescued you from futile thinking and narcissistic behavior. Through Jesus Christ, wear a new personality. Put on the knowledge that redemption from sin creates—the knowledge that your life is worth more effort than you were putting into it. Move your life upward!

You're renewed in another way, refurbished into God's likeness, his image. Paul closed his instruction about the new birth by telling the Colossians, "You've put on the new self, which is being renewed in the image of its Creator." In the past, before you knew Jesus as Savior and Lord, your character was godless. You may have been a decent neighbor, a welcome friend, a loyal citizen. But you were godless, without any resemblance to your Creator, and you didn't care about this deficiency! You looked first and foremost for the well-being of your spouse and children, for yourself, for your most-enjoyed relatives and a few close friends. Close, but not too intimate! Now that you know Jesus as the Deliverer from your wasted life, you're being re-made to reflect God's image which shines brightly in Jesus and brighter in yourself all the time. You're becoming a godly person.

When mending their ways, some people use pretty thin thread, don't they? It isn't long before the button comes off again or the patch pulls away from the sleeve. You've got to find strong thread if you want the tailoring job on your character to last beyond a few days. What's stronger than the character of Christ?

The motives of your behavior, since you met Jesus Christ, have begun to rise out of a changed heart. They reveal a new character within you. Paul commanded, "...as God's chosen people, holy and dearly loved, clothe yourselves with compassion, kindness, humility, gentleness and patience. Bear with each other and forgive whatever grievances you may have against one another. Forgive as the Lord forgave you. And over all these virtues put on love, which binds them all together in perfect unity" (Col. 3:12-14).

A difference between Christians and non-Christians is explained for me in the story of a grade school student who had trouble saying words with the letter *R* in them. As homework, his speech teacher gave him a sentence to practice. He was to repeat aloud ten times each night: "Robert gave Richard a rap in the rib for roasting the rabbit so rare."

After several days, the teacher decided to check the student's progress. The boy repeated: "Bob gave Dick a poke in the side for not cooking the bunny enough." He avoided the *R* words!

Isn't this the difference between Christians and non-Christians? Those who don't believe in Jesus avoid the *R* word—*rebirth*. The difference between a Christian and a non-Christian starts in an experience of grace which we call the new birth, or as some say, being born again. But new birth is only the beginning of the difference. Once you're reborn, your internal and external character changes. You do new things. You live in a new way. You live as Jesus Christ lived. His image is stamped on your soul.

Give this thought careful consideration: *Born anew in Christ, you're to live in a Christian way.* One touch of God's grace is a push in the right direction. Afterward, who you are, what you do, and how you speak has to be improved!

2
A SECOND TOUCH: COVENANT

How are you saved? By faith in Jesus Christ. Correct. But where's faith itself come from? Do you work it up in your heart? Do you reason it out in your head? Neither. The source of faith in Jesus isn't inside you. It's in God. He puts faith in your heart and mind, and this faith is the basis of his covenant with you and all Christians. Throughout scripture, the emphasis falls on God's activity, not human activity. As Paul wrote to the Ephesian believers, "...it is by grace you have been saved, through faith—and this not from yourselves, it is the gift of God—not by works, so that no one can boast" (Eph. 2:8-9).

In the ancient near east, covenants were agreements established by a strong king with dependent kings. The great king gave the terms of agreement and assumed responsibilities to lead and protect. Lesser rulers vowed loyalty and support. Giving you forgiveness and grace through his Son Jesus Christ, God assumes the role of the Great King and establishes a covenant with you. A covenant of grace. He agrees to be your sovereign Lord who leads and protects you. The best and only action you take in establishing the covenant is to pledge loyalty and support to the Lord.

As God's gracious palm is placed on your shoulder, he becomes the Lord, and you become the servant. Even your faith in Jesus is his gracious gift! The Lord has made a covenant with you, to be your God. Only by his grace are you saved. Only by his favor can you serve him. He needs nothing from you but asks everything good out of you.

By Grace You Are Saved

Twice, Paul emphasized this fact for the Ephesians. First, he wrote, "...because of his great love for us, God, who is rich in mercy, made us alive with Christ even when we were dead in transgressions—it is by grace you have been saved," and then he said, "...it is by grace you have been saved, through faith—and this not from yourselves, it is the gift of God—not by works, so that no one can boast" (Eph. 2:4-5, 8-9). Heaven's rich mercy does what you couldn't begin to do for yourself. Salvation arrives by the grace of God active in your life.

Mark Twain understood this truth about God's grace. He said, "Heaven goes by favor. If it went by merit, you would stay out, and your dog would go in!"

You can't merit salvation. You can't earn it in any way. There's nothing, not one thing, you can do to work your way into God's good graces. Why? Because you're a sinner like me! And no sinner deserves God's attention, only condemnation. Still, for some reason, he loves sinful people like us, and his love urges him to forgive and rescue us.

When Jesus put himself between us and the Father, he said, "Father, look what I did for this sinner. I died for him, for her." God's heart melts. He forgives your sin and accepts you back to himself.

Read Paul's declaration again: "...it is by grace you have been saved, through faith—and this not from yourselves, it is the gift of God—not by works, so that no one can boast" (Eph. 2:8-9). How wonderful! A truth you can cling to whenever doubt sinks onto your horizon!

By Grace, Through Faith

Stare at God's surprising hand for a while. How has it caressed your life? Consider your spiritual condition *before* you met Jesus. You busily added the disgusting bricks labeled hatred, envy, drunkenness, thievery and more to the wall separating you from your Father in heaven. You cemented it together with the mortar of selfishness. Paul described for his Ephesian friends the spiritual poverty of each human being who hasn't received Christ:

> "As for you, you were dead in your transgressions and sins, in which you used to live when you followed the ways of this world and of the ruler of the kingdom of the air, the spirit who is now at work in those who are disobedient. All of us also lived among them at one time, gratifying the cravings of our sinful nature and following its desires and thoughts. Like the rest, we were by nature objects of wrath" (Eph. 2:1-3).

What a wonder! God agreed to be our King, although our characters were steeped in sin. Hallelujah! The Lord is gracious! We are redeemed!

How did the Almighty overcome our deplorable spiritual condition? Again, Paul explained for believers at Ephesus:

> "And God raised us up with Christ and seated us with him in the heavenly realms in Christ Jesus, in order that in the coming ages he might show the incomparable riches of his grace, expressed in his kindness to us in Christ Jesus. For it is by grace you have been saved, through faith—and this not from yourselves, it is the gift of God—not by works, so that no one can boast" (Eph. 2:6-9).

Faith opened heaven's door, and faith is the key that unlocks your heart's door, too. Through it, God gave you access to himself, digging a channel through your dirt so that his awesome love might flow into you.

Repeatedly, Paul announced your Savior's identity. Because you believe in *Jesus*, you no longer obey the spirit at work in the hearts of all who disobey God. You serve a living Lord, who was crucified, dead and buried, but who is alive again, ruling your life as the Great King.

Standing alone on the edge of the Grand Canyon in Arizona, a man slipped. He hurtled over the edge. As he fell, he grabbed at rocks and bushes until finally he caught one. He breathed hard and shouted, "Is anybody up there?"

A voice from overhead answered, "There sure is."

The man answered, "Can you help me get back to the rim?"

"I sure can," the voice said.

"What do you need from me?" the man asked.

"Faith," the voice answered. "Trust me. Let go, and I'll save you."

The man breathed hard and shouted, "Is there anybody else up there?"

If the common assumption is true, then having faith in God is something you and I, and the man on the cliff, must *do*. But the truth is that God's covenant of salvation isn't based on anything you accomplish, not even believing. The Great King agrees to save you if you believe in him. Then he puts faith in you! Imagine this: *Even your faith in Jesus is God's gracious gift!*

Seems strange, huh? God's way of working out your salvation, of being your God, is via the faith he himself gives you. If this isn't what you expected, praise the Lord for his covenant of grace! It's more than you or I deserve. It *is* a gift!

By Grace, Not by Works

Don't your deeds count for anything? Yes, they do, but only *after* you're saved. Your deeds become the evidence that you were given faith in Jesus and were rescued through him. Once the divine finger points to the path, you're able to move along it in the knowledge that he chose it for you. As Paul told the Ephesians, "...we are God's workmanship, created in Christ Jesus to do good works, which God prepared in advance for us to do" (Eph. 2:10). *To do good works*. God had a reason for rescuing you. You're his work of art, his creation, and you're designed to glorify him by your activities, your manner of life. After God's gift of faith in Christ redeems you, your works become evidence of the grace within you.

When a powerful king made a covenant with a dependent king, the vassal was expected to serve the overlord. Loyalty and assistance were required. Vassals did what the great king asked. In God's covenant with you, you were created to do good; he prepared your tasks ahead of time. Your delivered life is lived by good deeds, but your status of being saved is received as a gracious gift. By his covenant touch, God's favor hands you the assignments he expects you to do. His favor comes before your service.

In America, it's a popular notion, among Christians as well as others, that the best place to find a helping hand is at the end of your own wrist! But Christianity teaches something harder to believe than this self-help way to a life worth living. It teaches absolute surrender to God in Christ. You can't do anything to gain redemption. It's a divine gift so that you, a mere human being, have nothing to boast about except the Lord himself. Once this is true, your Lord sets your feet to the path of servanthood and puts your hands to the task of spreading his mercy abroad in a world desperate to know he loves every creature in it.

As the spiritual guide of early Presbyterians, John Calvin said, "We are what we are completely by the grace of God." We have nothing in our personalities to make us good, holy or righteous. Christians live, move, have their being, and do useful deeds, because God works in them by grace. No Christian deserves the privilege, yet a loving Father bestows it. Amazing!

Throughout scripture, emphasis falls on heaven's activity, not human movement. Giving you grace and forgiveness through Jesus, God assumes the role of the Great King and establishes a covenant with you. It's an agreement to be your sovereign Lord who leads and protects you. The best action you take in establishing the covenant is to pledge loyalty and support to the Lord. "...it is by grace you have been saved, through faith—and this not from yourselves, it is the gift of God—not by works, so that no one can boast" (Eph. 2:8-9). Simply surrender yourself completely.

Mull over an overwhelming truth: *Your faith in Jesus is God's gracious gift!* The Lord made a covenant with you, to be your God. Only by his grace are you saved, and by it you can serve him where he needs you. In a world of pain, a world of lost souls eager to find their true home, you have gifts to share, gifts that open heaven's doors. The deeds you do for others signal that you're a disciple of the Nazarene.

Are you committed to serve the Great King?

3
A THIRD TOUCH:
REPENTANCE

Patrick O'Reilly was on his deathbed, and the family called for the priest. When the priest administered last rites, he asked O'Reilly, "Do you repent of your sins and renounce the world, the flesh and the devil?"

O'Reilly answered, "Really now, Father, do ya' t'ink it wise in me condition to go offendin' one so powerful as the divil himself?"

I've met people who fear the "devil himself," and I conclude that their real problem lies in acknowledging what *repentance* means for them. Repentance means turning to God through faith in Jesus Christ; then you must demonstrate your repentance by your deeds. Many want salvation without a significant change in their behavior, but God wants a complete repentance that involves heart, mind, and conduct.

Examine another touch of grace: *repentance*.

An Inferior Repentance

The kind of repentance many seek to give the Lord is an inferior kind. They think no sorrow, shame or contrition is necessary.

The apostle Paul was like this before he surrendered to Christ. Before Festus and Agrippa, he confessed: "I too was convinced that I ought to do all that was possible to oppose the name of Jesus of Nazareth. And that is just what I did in Jerusalem. On the authority of the chief priests I put many of the saints in prison, and when they were put to death, I cast my vote against them. Many a time I went from one synagogue to another to have them punished, and I tried to force them to blaspheme. In my obsession against them, I even went to foreign cities to persecute them" (Acts 26:9-11).

Denying you have bad attitudes toward God, toward people, toward yourself, you see no need to repent, to ask forgiveness, or to give it. Such a man was Paul the apostle before his call to discipleship.

Other people admit they've sinned, but they excuse themselves. They say, "Everybody does a few wrong things. I'm no worse than the average sinner." By this thought they deny that sin is real. It's just how society views things. They think they're free to choose a taboo action as long as they don't hurt others or the community as a whole. Some people consider sin to be self-fulfillment. "As long as it makes you feel satisfied, go ahead! Do it! Enjoy yourself! But only if you're not uncomfortable doing it! It's best to avoid it then. Don't consider it wrong because somebody else tells you it's wrong. Fulfill yourself as a person. You'll be okay." With all sorts of evasive thoughts about sin and denials of the need to change, people give the Lord either a shallow repentance or no repentance at all.

Why do we give an inferior repentance? Because we forget to trust God to help us repent. We don't think God truly cares. But, as the apostle Paul discovered, the Lord does care. Read his own testimony:

> "On one of these journeys I was going to Damascus with the authority and commission of the chief priests. About noon, O king, as I was on the road, I saw a light from heaven, brighter than the sun, blazing around me and my companions. We all fell to the ground, and I heard a voice saying to me in Aramaic, 'Saul, Saul, why do you persecute me? It is hard for you to kick against the goads.'
>
> "Then I asked, 'Who are you, Lord?'
>
> "'I am Jesus, whom you are persecuting,' the Lord replied. 'Now get up and stand on your feet. I have appeared to you to appoint you as a servant and as a

witness of what you have seen of me and what I will show you. I will rescue you from your own people and from the Gentiles. I am sending you to them to open their eyes and turn them from darkness to light, and from the power of Satan to God, so that they may receive forgiveness of sins and a place among those who are sanctified by faith in me'" (Acts 26:12-18).

Human beings tend to believe their characters are fairly decent, and they don't need to repent of any real sins. So they spend their time polishing a reputation. But remember what a wise man said: "If you spend too much time polishing your reputation, your character will get tarnished!"

Learn that the Lord Jesus loves you and wants to make you better than you've been. You need his touch of repentance. Seek the gentle tap of his fingers on your heart every day. Through his Spirit and his word, he'll pinpoint your trouble spots. Start with an honest attitude about yourself. Admit that you've sinned.

A Superior Repentance

Repentance means turning to God through faith in Jesus Christ. Every believer seems to understand and practice this return to the Lord. They inspect their lives daily, analyzing themselves to see where they fall short in being like Jesus. Then they confess their sins and other inadequacies, asking to be made more like their Master. They renounce the world, the flesh and the devil in order to be made new creatures by the Holy Spirit, who instructs and guides them. Yet, sooner or later, Christians realize they can't mold a likeness to Christ into their character or behavior under their own power. You must have God's gracious touch to help you into repentance and to turn you away from sin to the Savior.

The apostle Paul found such help on the road into Damascus, and he discovered at the same moment the Lord Jesus' willingness to help all people. As the risen one told his new apostle about the Gentiles among whom he'd serve: "I am sending you to them to open their eyes and turn them from darkness to light, and from the power of Satan to God, so that they may receive forgiveness of sins and a place among those who are sanctified by faith in me" (Acts 26:17*b*-18). Gentiles required God's grace to believe, repent, and turn toward the Redeemer, and the apostle Paul was commissioned to take the Lord's forgiving grace to them. Like him, you have an appointment to a ministry of touching others with the gospel.

Vance Havner defined repentance as "a change of mind about sin and self and Savior." It's a change in thinking about sin, because you admit sin is real. You confess you've committed sin. Repentance is a change in your thoughts about yourself, because you know you stand in constant need of heaven's grace and help. Repentance is a change in your opinion about the Savior, because you learn how he brings you the grace you must have every day to live as he desires. Isn't this a superior repentance?

A Superb Repentance

A superb repentance is better yet. Turning to God through faith in Jesus Christ, you could demonstrate your repentance by your deeds. This would raise the quality of your sorrow and remorse for having transgressed. Once more, it's beyond your ability to perform a superb penitence, to make your deeds good all the time. You require God's gracious nudge to carry you beyond your ability to improve your behavior.

The apostle Paul's experience of grace in repentance is, again, a good presentation of how Jesus takes hold on a life, changes it for the better, then uses it to create traction for one's walk in a slippery world. Paul explained to the king, "So then, King Agrippa, I was not disobedient to the vision from heaven. First to those in Damascus, then to those in Jerusalem and in all Judea, and to the Gentiles also, I preached that they should repent and turn to God and prove their repentance by their deeds" (Acts 26:19-20). Turning away from sin means turning toward holiness and righteousness. Your deeds must improve!

Henry Ward Beecher, said, "Repentance may begin instantly, but reformation often requires a sphere of years." In other words, after a changed life comes the living of that changed life. You cannot simply say, "Forgive me, Lord!" and walk away feeling good. You have to rearrange the places you go, the things you say, and what you seek to do. Plus, the renovation isn't short-term or limited in scope. Repentance has to lead to improvement of your entire character, all your commitments, and your attitude toward yourself, others, and God. Such refurbishing demands years of intense labor and sacrifice under the guidance of the Holy Spirit and the teachings of Christ.

Will you give God the repentance he wants? His hand is on your shoulder to comfort and direct you. Perhaps you've always thought you didn't need to feel regrets. Jesus' death on the cross nullified all the bad you once did. True, to a point, but you still have to alter your conduct from selfishness to surrender, from anger to acceptance, from carelessness to kindness. Contrition demands obedience to the holy standards the Almighty places on repentant sinners.

You were a fairly decent person before you knew Christ as Savior. Most people are, from a human point of view. But examine yourself closely. Is there a new sin you should turn away from? You've wanted to change for years, but the snake keeps lifting its head. Perhaps the time has come to drive it back into the woods and out of your yard. Repent, then walk away from it. Walk back toward God with Jesus at your side. Behave in a better way from now on. Refuse to do the old habits of sin, and start to learn new habits of goodness. Offer your Master a superb repentance.

Contemplate what God's gracious touch means for your regular activities. Repentance means turning to God through faith in Jesus Christ, but then you should demonstrate repentance by what you do, where you go, and how you speak to others. Handle others with the grace God used to stroke your soul.

4
A FOURTH TOUCH:
LOYAL RELATIONSHIPS

Maybe you're like me. A bit mystified. You'd think the church would be popular in this day and age. With all the stress on solid relationships, the church ought to be the place to go, because churches have always gotten blue ribbons for building bonds between people. We aren't perfect about it, mind you, but we've always had pretty good grades in this subject. Yet people dismiss churches as places where they can find both friends and loyalty. I conclude that either churches aren't as good at relationships as I thought or people don't want truly significant companionship with others.

Take stock of a maturing Christian life. The apostle Paul spoke about it to Timothy. His lesson was simple: *Loyal relationships are part and parcel of the covenant community's experience of God's grace.*

Pastor and People

Paul suggested that the pastoral relationship is part of a covenant community's experience of God's grace. He told Timothy: "Do not rebuke an older man harshly, but exhort him as if he were your father. Treat younger men as brothers, older women as mothers, and younger women as sisters, with absolute purity" (1 Tim. 5:1-2).

As head of the church where he ministered, Timothy was called to bring his people close enough to Christ that the Lord's hand might rest on them. He should treat church members with respect and consideration. When older men or women needed correction, he was charged to plead with them as if appealing to a parent. Younger folks were to be treated as one sibling is supposed to treat another, with purity and compassion. The grace a pastor experiences from the Lord ought to spill over into the way he treats church members.

A minister came out of a ten-year retirement to preach for a small country church. The first Sunday in the pulpit a young couple invited him to dinner. While they were in the kitchen, the pastor was in the living room with their son. He asked the boy if he knew what they were having for dinner.

The boy said, "A goat."

"A goat?" the pastor asked. "Are you sure?"

"Yep, I heard Dad tell Mom, 'We might as well get it over with and have the old goat for dinner.'"

It may not always be easy to be gracious, but your relationship with your pastor is part of the covenant community's experience of God's touch.

Family Relations

Paul also suggested that family relationships are part of the covenant community's experience of the Lord's favor. He wrote to Timothy:

> ...if a widow has children or grandchildren, these should learn first of all to put their religion into practice by caring for their own family and so repaying their parents and grandparents, for this is pleasing to God. ...Give the people these instructions, too, so that no one may be open to blame. If anyone does not provide for his relatives, and especially for his immediate family, he has denied the faith and is worse than an unbeliever.
>
> ...
>
> If any woman who is a believer has widows in her family, she should help them and not let the church be burdened with them, so that the church can help those widows who are really in need (1 Tim. 5:4, 7-8, 16).

Care for widows was a special concern in the ancient church because women without husbands were at the mud level of society. They had few means of support and often died of malnutrition or disease. Many widows joined churches, and the congregations gave them aid and shelter. Paul felt Christians with widows in their families were obligated to help them before the church stepped in. This way a church could spread its resources further when helping the destitute. (Budget problems existed back then, too!) So Paul told Timothy to teach the congregation about their duty toward the elderly. Faith and family intersect in practical ways.

On the Sunday when Pittsburgh's Three Rivers Stadium was imploded, I heard about a widow who went to every Steelers home game with her husband. At the last game she attended, a man next to her noticed an empty seat and remarked about it. "My husband's seat," she answered tersely, "but he died."

The man asked her, "Isn't there another family member who could use the seat?"

"I suppose so," the widow said, "but they're all at the funeral!"

Don't get your priorities mixed up! Faith and family obligations come together clearly. Family relationships are part of the covenant community's experience of God's caressing hand. When we fail to apply grace to those we love, bad things happen. When we share with them God's favor in Christ, bad times are weathered. At the very least, we don't struggle through life's storms alone.

Church Relations

Paul suggested that church relationships also express God's embrace of his covenant community. He wrote to Timothy:

"Give proper recognition to those widows who are really in need. ...The widow who is really in need and left all alone puts her hope in God and continues night and day to pray and to ask God for help. But the widow who lives for pleasure is dead even while she lives" (1 Tim. 5:3, 5-6).

Some widows in the ancient church had genuine needs. They counted on only God and the church for help. No one else was available to them! Timothy was counseled to make certain destitute women received help from the followers of Christ. Good relationships in the church demanded nothing less from a congregation.

A student told her Sunday school teacher about her grandparents' fiftieth anniversary. The teacher said, "Your grandparents are lucky to have such a long life together."

"Oh, it wasn't luck," the girl answered. "Grandma said she had to do a lot of work on Grandpa!"

Good relationships take a lot of work. This includes relationships in a congregation. When we work at them diligently, we receive unexpected hugs from God. But it requires exertion, discipline, which Christians sometimes won't give to their associations within the congregation.

Alexander MacLaren told his congregation, "The self-denial and persistence and concentration which are freely spent upon excellence in athletic pursuits might well put to shame the way in which Christians go about the task of 'doing' their religion."

Isn't this especially true regarding relations with other members? Christ's disciples are quick to judge or condemn others in his body and slow to restore relations after being hard-pressed by miffed feelings, disagreement or misunderstanding. Churches long for spiritual athletes, who train vigorously and constantly in the ability to build solid and wholesome fellowship among members. Neglect love's disciplines, such as patience and kindness, and they miss the stroke of the Lord's fingers on the church's hand. They miss the divine love which excels all loves.

Widows in the Church

Finally, Paul suggested that a widow's relationship to the church is part of God's desire to cuddle the covenant community. He told Timothy:

> No widow may be put on the list of widows unless she is over sixty, has been faithful to her husband, and is well known for her good deeds, such as bringing up children, showing hospitality, washing the feet of the saints, helping those in trouble and devoting herself to all kinds of good deeds.
>
> As for younger widows, do not put them on such a list. For when their sensual desires overcome their dedication to Christ, they want to marry. Thus they bring judgment on themselves, because they have broken their first pledge. Besides, they get into the habit of being idle and going about from house to house. And not only do they become idlers, but also gossips and busybodies, saying things they ought not to. So I counsel younger widows to marry, to have children, to manage their homes and to give the enemy no opportunity for slander. Some have in fact already turned away to follow Satan. (1 Tim. 5:9-15).

All relationships are two way. Widows in the ancient church owed the church a holy life. They ministered to others in the fellowship, but they weren't to become busybodies, nor to gossip. To experience God's grace, widows had to govern their conduct well.

Some widows in the ancient church may have been like a woman with a troubled marriage. She called one of those telephone psychics and asked for advice. The psychic told her, "Prepare yourself for widowhood. Your husband is about to die a violent death."

The caller sighed and asked, "Will I be acquitted?"

Too much time on your hands or too much frustration can lead to unholy behavior. Like widows in the ancient church, you and I need to govern how we live in order to bring honor to our Lord Jesus Christ. If we do this, we discover that loyal relationships are part of the covenant community's experience of the poignant touch of God's grace.

Meditate for a while on a useful truth of good discipleship: *Loyal relationships are part and parcel of the covenant community's experience of God's grace.*

5
A FIFTH TOUCH:
CALLING

Throughout your lifetime, you receive all kinds of calls, don't you? The mail arrives, and a small card invites you to a party. A man knocks on the door, and hands you a summons to appear in court. The phone rings, and your sister's voice urges you to stop what you're doing and listen to her most recent woes. If you use the internet, you might receive a call through your computer and speak long distance with video for little or no cost. Your cell phone rings a lot! Regardless how they arrive, you get many calls in your lifetime. Each one enlists your action.

There's one call you receive that's more important than any other. The call comes from God through Jesus Christ. As the apostle Paul explained, "God, who has called you into fellowship with his Son Jesus Christ our Lord, is faithful" (1 Cor. 1:9). Your faithful God has called you into fellowship with his Son, the Lord Jesus Christ. Are you being asked to believe? to renew your commitment? to grow into a higher level off Christian spiritual life? What action are you asked take? When God calls, he expects you to answer by deeds of service or love.

Reflect on this for a while.

Your Faithful God

Your God is faithful. Paul offered an explanation to Corinthian believers. He wrote a little about the Lord's faithfulness toward them: "I always thank God for you because of his grace given you in Christ Jesus. For in him you have been enriched in every way—in all your speaking and in all your knowledge—because our testimony about Christ was confirmed in you" (1 Cor. 1:4-6).

When Paul witnessed to the Corinthians, they believed his message about Jesus. God confirmed it by his finger of grace, by giving them knowledge of his Son and by the apostle's ability to witness about Christ Jesus. The Almighty confirmed his call to the Corinthian believers by enriching them spiritually. God does these things for you, too, and they prove his faithfulness toward you. Because you believe the gospel, you're tapped by grace and able to receive and give a witness about your Savior. How faithful God is!

Because God is faithful, our trust has to be more in him than in ourselves, in what he does more than anything we can do.

A visitor to the White House during the Civil War commented to Abraham Lincoln that the citizens of his state believed the Union's welfare depended on God and Mr. Lincoln. The president nodded, then said, "Well, my friend, you are half correct."

Temptation is strong to think we trust Christ with everything while holding back our full surrender to his guidance. We're convinced of our skill and tactics. We believe we're able to extricate ourselves from almost any situation if provided with time, money, friends or information, with whatever we deem necessary for us to locate solutions. In truth, we require little more than an awareness that our Master is completely dependable coupled with our surrender to his control. Living in Jesus, we must abide in him in order to be productive disciples. God's our greatest resource in life, death, health, relationships, in everything.

I love reading letters kids write to God. Recently, I found the following letters which show how profound children's questions about God can be.

Dear God, Why do people have to die? You keep having to make new ones. So why not keep the ones you got already? *Sammy.*

Dear Lord: Did you really want a giraffe to look like it does? Or were they a accident? *Joan.*

O God! Don't worry bout me. I always look both ways. *Jimmy.*

Dearest God, I didn't like orange or purple together. Until I saw the sunset you made last night. It was neat! *Louisa.*

What are your questions about God? Remember: He's faithful toward you and teaches you about himself and his ways.

Still, a question lingers: *How can you be certain God is faithful?*

Your Fellowship with Jesus

Isn't the answer clear? You know God's faithful, because he called you into an abiding and abundant fellowship with his Son Jesus. Surely, his dependability is exhibited in his call for you to know, enjoy and serve him. A Christian's calling is closely tied to God as the trustworthy Lord.

Again, Paul explained to the Corinthian believers a little about their fellowship with the faithful Jesus. He wrote, "...you do not lack any spiritual gift as you eagerly wait for our Lord Jesus Christ to be revealed. He will keep you strong to the end, so that you will be blameless on the day of our Lord Jesus Christ" (1 Cor. 1:7-8). If you know Jesus, then you have spiritual gifts, and you understand how to use the gifts until Jesus returns. You comprehend that Christ keeps you strong until the end comes. He maintains you as a blameless disciple. You trust Jesus because you have fellowship with him daily, and this friendship assures you of his trustworthiness.

A Japanese college student in the United States met Christians and through them learned to know Jesus as Savior. While he prepared to return home, he confided in a friend. "It's a strange thing," he said. "When you come into fellowship with Jesus, you cannot ever get away from him.

You don't want to lose him because you know only he is dependable."

The Christian life isn't always easy. This Japanese believer had to return to his family's home where Jesus wasn't honored. He'd soon find himself tested and, maybe, assaulted for his faith. You aren't promised an easy life in Christ. As he warned his disciples, "If the world hates you, keep in mind that it hated me first" (Jn. 15:18). Until he returns, you'll be tempted to give up the faith or at least let its flame cool down until it barely gives off heat or light. A daily fellowship with Jesus will keep you blameless until he arrives. You can trust him, and if you do, he'll make you strong.

Albert Schweitzer, the Nobel-winning missionary, wrote about a Christian's friendship with Jesus of Nazareth: "…to those who obey him, whether they be wise or simple, he will reveal himself in the toils, the conflicts, the sufferings which they shall pass through in his fellowship, and, as an ineffable mystery, they shall learn in their own experience who he is." The best way to discover the dependability of Christ is to answer his call to become his companion and to serve others as he leads you. Schweitzer lived in this way. No reason exists that you cannot do so, too.

Another question lingers in the mind. *What's so important about Jesus?*

Your Lord Jesus

"Tell me your picture of Jesus," Oscar Pfister said, "and I'll tell you important facts about your own character." Jesus is important because your opinion of him reveals your personality. Who you are is directly related to what you love or hate about Jesus Christ.

Once again, the apostle Paul gave the details to the Corinthians. He wrote about their Lord Jesus: "God, who has called you into fellowship with his Son Jesus Christ our Lord, is faithful" (1 Cor. 1:9). The one who calls you cannot be ignored. Jesus is important for two reasons: He is God's faithful Son, and he is also your dependable Lord.

Jean Jacques Rousseau wrote about Jesus' divinity. "If the life and death of Socrates were those of a man," he said, "the life and death of Jesus were those of a God." Christ's experience among us humans displayed his divine character while he accomplished his mission of both teaching us and dying for us. He lived with us, revealing the Father, and he died only to rise again, proving himself mysteriously to be God, too.

Have you heard of anyone else dying and at the same moment asking God to forgive his executioners? It may have happened but not so dramatically as with Jesus, and probably it happened after his example was given. Have you heard of anyone else rising from the dead though his grave was sealed and guarded by soldiers? Have you heard of anyone else appearing to twelve disciples in a locked upper room, or being seen by five hundred people over several weeks after he died and was resurrected? All these things happened to Jesus. His life and death is God's life and death. He's the divine Son. Dare you forget or neglect to relate yourself to him?

Consider Jesus also as your Lord. The idea of lordship is unpopular in today's world, at least in the United States. Our culture, especially since the Civil War, has steeped us in the thought that we're free to be what we choose, to do as we please. No one is our taskmaster. We allow no lords to reign over us. But the Nazarene insists on claiming authority over you. He calls you to submit to his wisdom and direction, his sovereignty. God touches your life when Christ calls you to surrender allegiance to him first and foremost.

A man who lived in Brazil never went to church, but he'd seen many statues and paintings of Jesus. He'd seen priests and altar boys parade through streets carrying a crucifix on religious holidays. One day, the man was asked, "Who is Jesus?"

"I'm not sure," he said. "I guess he's that dead man on a stick."

When you don't know him as Savior and Lord, Jesus is only an interesting man whom others honor, but to you he's little more than a dead man hammered onto a stick!

As a Christian, you're summoned into fellowship with Jesus, but what action do you take regarding him? Do you believe with all your heart, mind, and strength that he calls you to discipleship? Do you trust God when your faith falters a bit? Do you seek the fellowship of the Son, your Lord, every day? Your faithful God has called you into fellowship with his Son, the Lord Jesus Christ. What actions are you taking now in response to the invitation to be touched by his grace?

6
A SIXTH TOUCH:
COMMUNION

In his book *The Joy of Living*, television weatherman Willard Scott wrote about a childhood experience with the Lord's Supper. When he was twelve, his family attended a Baptist church. Communion was served with grape juice in small plastic cups. Scott liked the juice and always tried to get every last drop out of the tiny container.

Once, a vacuum formed inside the cup, and his tongue was imprisoned in the plastic. He tried to yank the cup off, but it wouldn't come loose!

Suddenly the pastor announced a hymn, "Blest Be the Tie that Binds," asking everybody to hold hands! Just as quickly, worshipers on either side of the boy grabbed his fingers. Fearing discovery and parental discipline, young Scott was inspired. He sucked the whole cup into his mouth! After the singing ended, he was able to tug the offending cup off.

Consider the hidden adventure of faith known as the Lord's Supper as well as the deeper experience called *communion*. In this sacrament, Jesus Christ gives us fellowship with himself and makes us better people. Communion, also, is an experience of God's gracious and mysterious touch.

The apostle Paul highlighted the weighty meaning of communion when he penned these words: "Now the Lord is the Spirit, and where the Spirit of the Lord is, there is freedom. And we, who with unveiled faces all reflect the Lord's glory, are being transformed into his likeness with ever-increasing glory, which comes from the Lord, who is the Spirit" (2 Cor. 3:17-18).

What was Paul talking about? How does God's grace and favor reach us through this sacrament?

Communion

Through Jesus' institution of a holy supper, God set up a communion meal with his New Testament people. Through Moses, he'd inaugurated a similar dinner with his earlier people, the Passover. But a different sort of communion was also established then.

While the Israelites were in the desert at Mount Sinai, Moses ascended the mountain to receive the law. The commandments established a covenant by which the Jewish nation would live. The people would be the Lord's people, and he'd be their God. When Moses came down from the divine presence, his face shined with reflected glory. In time the reflection faded. Each time he returned to the people, Moses' shining face frightened them. He wore a veil to hide the lingering glory. God's covenant made by Moses' law became a communion, a fellowship, between the Lord and his people. They were one in mind and feeling.

Betsy asked her Sunday School teacher, "Did Moses ever get better?"

"What do you mean?" Mrs. Jones said.

"Well," Betsy explained, "last week you told us the Lord gave Moses two tablets!"

On tablets of stone, the Lord engraved his covenant and started a communion with his first people which was intended to create a healthy spiritual life for them and their children generation after generation.

In Jesus Christ, on the Mount of Transfiguration, three disciples were privileged to see a similar sight in Jesus' reflection of divine glory. They left the place in awe and wonder. As time passed, Jesus was crucified then resurrected. The earliest Christians meditated on the surpassing glory reflected in Jesus' life, death and rising. A new covenant was established with God's second people—Christian people, you and me. Again, with the new covenant in Christ came new fellowship.

The apostle Paul compared the two experiences of communion. He wrote to the Corinthian believers: "Now if the ministry that brought death, which was engraved in letters on stone, came with glory, so that the Israelites could not look steadily at the face of Moses because of its glory, fading though it was, will not the ministry of the Spirit be even more glorious? If the ministry that condemns men is glorious, how much more glorious is the ministry that brings righteousness! For what was glorious has no glory now in comparison with the surpassing glory. And if what was fading away came with glory, how much greater is the glory of that which lasts!" (2 Cor. 3:7-11)

The law given through Moses served as a teacher by instructing the Israelites how to please God. It also served as a police officer by protecting them against sin when they obeyed and by punishing sin when they disobeyed. This was a glorious service for God's first covenant people. Then in Jesus Christ, who brought God's touch of grace to a second covenant people, a greater glory was revealed. This glory is unfading and lasts for eternity. Alleluia! Praise God for wanting fellowship with us!

Explore the deeper meaning of the Lord's Supper: *In grace, God sets up his communion with us, his newest people.* We did not deserve the sacrament, but the Lord established it as a way to touch us often.

Character

But there's more!

By allowing his grace to trace itself in their hearts, God restored a godly character in his earliest people. The purpose of Moses' Law was to make God's people holy, and for countless numbers of them, it did so. Israelites within every generation have lived godly, righteous lives. Yet the divinely appointed law wasn't completely successful in reaching the entire populous of the covenant people. As Paul admitted, "…their minds were made dull, for to this day the same veil remains when the old covenant is read. It has not been removed, because only in Christ is it taken away" (2 Cor. 3:14).

This isn't a condemnation of every Jewish individual, but only those who refused to understand God's intent and design for the Old Testament way of life, whom the Old Testament prophets themselves criticized. We must never forget that many who followed the first covenant faithfully displayed the Lord's glory in their godly characters.

In a similar way, by grace, God restores Christ's character within us, his newest people. As the apostle Paul explained, "Now the Lord is the Spirit, and where the Spirit of the Lord is, there is freedom. And we, who with unveiled faces all reflect the Lord's glory, are being transformed into his likeness with ever-increasing glory, which comes from the Lord, who is the Spirit" (2 Cor. 3:17-18).

When people walk through life in communion with Jesus, they become like him. This is true in all human associations; the more people are around each other, learning and serving together, the more likeminded they become. A Christian's holy, righteous behavior is an expression of God's glory discovered in Christ's face. Here's the deeper meaning of communion—*fellowship with the Lord Most High*.

Perhaps this is what bothers you about some who say they love Jesus Christ. The fruit of his character is missing from their daily conduct. They seem not to live in communion with Christ. You see it in their church activities. Their tempers are quick when they disagree with other board members, or they're hasty in what they think the congregation ought to do in its mission or witness. We learn early in our Christian growth that our souls and actions are supposed to mesh seamlessly. When other believers falter, we question their integrity.

Be careful when this happens to you. Righteousness and ungodliness live together in the same soul, whether it's yours or mine. Each Christian is a strange mixture of growth and decay. The process of becoming like Jesus Christ is a lifelong adventure in self-discovery, change, failure and maturity. Therefore, it's a matter of growth through suffering.

Pope Pius XII spoke about the value of suffering for Christians: "The life and sufferings of our Savior, the pains which so many great men have born and even sought and through which they have matured and risen to the summits of Christian heroism, the daily examples we see of acceptance of the cross with resignation: all this reveals the meaning of suffering, of the patient acceptance of pain in the present plan of salvation, for the duration of this earthly life."

Such insight makes us slower to write other believers out of God's script. He's never finished improving them, just as he always mends our brokenness. Your troublesome friends at church may yet mature through the struggles within their souls and conduct.

At a rural Presbyterian Church, the pastor noted a loose board on the building. He fetched a hammer to fasten it in place. While he pounded, a boy watched intently. After the pastor finished, he asked the young fellow, "Did you want a lesson in carpentry?"

"No," the boy said, "I just wanted to hear what a preacher says when he hits his thumb!"

Not only is a preacher supposed to show himself to be a better person because he was tapped by grace, but every Christian personality should improve because of fellowship with Jesus. Your daily communion with him through scripture reading and prayer ought to spark in you an awareness that you're not alone in the affairs of faith and obedience. When Christ calls you to a task, he lends a hand to accomplish it. He brings heavenly resources to your assigned project or insurmountable problem. Christians are neither orphans nor destitute! They commune with the Master.

Do you understand what Paul was saying? Do you see how God gives you fellowship with himself and makes you a better person?

Mull over Paul's words again: "Now the Lord is the Spirit, and where the Spirit of the Lord is, there is freedom. And we, who with unveiled faces all reflect the Lord's glory, are being transformed into his likeness with ever-increasing glory, which comes from the Lord, who is the Spirit" (2 Cor. 3:17-18).

Reach out to the Lord Jesus Christ, to God the Father, to the Holy Spirit. Receive the grace your Lord has for you. Know this: *God gives you fellowship with himself and makes you a better person.* Isn't this why he touches you with his grace?

BOOK TWO
THE FLAWLESS WORD

The sayings of Agur son of Jakeh—an oracle:

This man declared to Ithiel,
    to Ithiel and to Ucal:
"I am the most ignorant of men;
    I do not have a man's understanding.
I have not learned wisdom,
    nor have I knowledge of the Holy One.
Who has gone up to heaven and come down?
    Who has gathered up the wind in the hollow of his
        hands?
Who has wrapped up the waters in his cloak?
    Who has established all the ends of the earth?
What is his name, and the name of his son?
    Tell me if you know!

"Every word of God is flawless;
    he is a shield to those who take refuge in him.
Do not add to his words,
    or he will rebuke you and prove you a liar.

"Two things I ask of you, O Lord;
    do not refuse me before I die:
Keep falsehood and lies far from me;
    give me neither poverty nor riches,
    but give me only my daily bread.
Otherwise, I may have too much and disown you
    and say, 'Who is the Lord?'
Or I may become poor and steal,
    and so dishonor the name of my God."

Proverbs 30:1-9

1
THE FLAWLESS WORD

Every word of God is flawless;
> he is a shield to those who take refuge in him.
Do not add to his words,
> or he will rebuke you and prove you a liar.

Proverbs 30:5-6

A ship's captain stood on the bridge. He bellowed orders to the crew, but before shouting, he always opened a small wooden box and looked inside. The crew wondered what he had in the box. One day while the captain was ashore, a sailor stole into the captain's quarters, found the box, and opened it. Inside lay a slip of paper, and on it were the words: "Port means *left*. Starboard means *right*."

As much as we want to recall some information, it's just hard to remember. This is true even in the knowledge of ourselves and Jesus Christ. An author of Proverbs who was named Agur thought about this dilemma and asked his students, "Who's gone into heaven and brought down a good understanding of human beings or of God?" The sage implied that no one had gone there, yet he described how the flawless word of God gives us the understanding we seek. His conclusion is a helpful thought that we should work to remember: *Knowing God is an experience of those who trust his word.*

৪৩৫৪

In thinking about this, let's first consider the nature of the Bible. The Bible is God's flawless word. Many people argue that the Holy Book isn't without mistakes. For instance, it says the earth is flat. Critics declare—and they're right—that scientific details in scripture have been proven impossible. Yet listen again to Agur's thought: "Every word of God is flawless…" (Prov. 30:5*a*). What does the word *flawless* suggest? Flawless means the Bible's intact. It's accurate and error-free. But how can a shadow back up a flight of stairs without the earth changing its rotation? Many bits and pieces of Holy Writ are held out as proof of biblical errors. Still, scientific data change. Our own generation has altered its acceptance of old theories over and over because of new experiments and new details. But the Bible is not a science textbook; it's a religious book, about the relations between God and people, between you and Jesus. In those respects, it's error-free. The human heart and the Lord's heart are clearly, accurately, correctly revealed. It's the flawless word of God.

Agur highlighted another aspect of its nature. The Bible is God's worthwhile word. The sage wrote, "…[God] is a shield to those who take refuge in him" (Prov. 30:5*b*). Your emergencies switch and adjust day after day, and as you read and re-read it, the Bible becomes God's protective cloak enfolding you. It's worth the effort to master its message. It keeps you safe and guides your behavior.

Cecil B. DeMille, who cast Charleton Heston as Moses in *The Ten Commandments*, explained his love of the Bible. "After more than sixty years of almost daily reading of the Bible," he said, "I never fail to find it always new and marvelously in tune with the changing needs of every day." God's word is flawless.

☙❧

Now, consider the reason for the Bible. The Bible instructs you in who *you* are. Again, in the book of Proverbs, Agur wrote,

Do not add to his words,

or he will rebuke you and prove you a liar.
Proverbs 30:6

The average human being constantly adds to God's word. We don't like what Jesus said about loving enemies, so we invent ways to re-define who our enemies are. Doing so, we become (from God's perspective) liars. "Proof-texting" is a favorite pastime for a lot of people. Think up a good idea, find a scripture verse that seems to support it, take the passage out of context, and declare, "The Bible teaches us thus and so!" Why do people do this? Because it allows them, temporarily, to avoid the truth about themselves, but abuse of the Bible amounts to adding to God's word, and opens you to his charge: "Liar!"

The Bible instructs you in who you are. This can be a positive lesson, too. You read the New Testament and discover yourself to be a redeemed sinner, who was picked out of a mud-pit by Jesus Christ and placed among his people. The Bible exists to teach you that the Holy Spirit gives you spiritual gifts and calls you into God's service within the fellowship of the church or in the larger community surrounding it. Lesson after lesson in scripture makes you a better person. You learn patience, kindness, self-surrender, humility, and many other virtues. You're taught how to stand firm when life's hard and how to support others who are lonely or who serve Jesus where you cannot serve him. The Bible instructs you in who you are.

The Bible also instructs you in who God is. As the wise teacher Agur wrote in Proverbs,

I am the most ignorant of men;
I do not have a man's understanding.
I have not learned wisdom,
nor have I knowledge of the Holy One.
Who has gone up to heaven and come down?
Who has gathered up the wind in the hollow of his hands?

Who has wrapped up the waters in his cloak?
    Who has established all the ends of the earth?
What is his name, and the name of his son?
    Tell me if you know!

Proverbs 30:2-4

God isn't the ogre people want to believe he is. He's the compassionate Creator who "gathered up the wind in the hollow of his hands," who blows away winter clouds and summer storms. He "wrapped up the waters in his cloak," protecting earth's water supply. God is with us, and we're blessed. Agur didn't know it, but God's the one who came down from heaven to earth, in his Son Jesus, and rescued us from sin and death. Jesus was the one who commanded wind and waves, "Quiet! Be still!" Again and again, the Bible teaches you who God is.

Theologian Emil Brunner explained, "The first and most important thing we know about God is that we know nothing about him except what he himself makes known." The reason we have the Bible is our ignorance about ourselves and God. He has to tell us who we are and who he is! So he gave us his flawless word. Knowing God is an experience of those who trust his word.

For this reason, shouldn't you sacrifice time from less important matters and read part of the Bible daily? As time goes on, the word of God builds up in you an understanding of God in Christ Jesus and a knowledge of how you relate to the Lord. Won't you give half an hour a day to understand and hear from the Creator who loves you?

Jesus said,

When a strong man, fully armed, guards his own house, his possessions are safe. But when someone stronger attacks and overpowers him, he takes away the armor in which the man trusted and divides up the spoils.

"He who is not with me is against me, and he who does not gather with me, scatters.

"When an evil spirit comes out of a man, it goes through arid places seeking rest and does not find it. Then it says, 'I will return to the house I left.' When it arrives, it finds the house swept clean and put in order. Then it goes and takes seven other spirits more wicked than itself, and they go in and live there. And the final condition of that man is worse than the first."

As Jesus was saying these things, a woman in the crowd called out, "Blessed is the mother who gave you birth and nursed you."

He replied, "Blessed rather are those who hear the word of God and obey it."

Luke 11:21-28

2

The Word Obeyed

...a woman in the crowd called out, "Blessed is the mother
who gave you birth and nursed you."

He replied, "Blessed rather are those who hear the
word of God and obey it."

Luke 11:27-28

People seek happiness in a variety of ways. Some look for
happiness in their family circle, but not everybody seeks it in
strong kinship ties. George Burns said: "Happiness is having
a large, loving, caring, close-knit family in another city." Or
as someone else put it: "School days are the happiest days in
your life, if your kids are old enough to go." Freedom from
family duty can seem like a blessing, but most people
treasure their families—according to one survey, even above
good health or a satisfying job.

But I've found that happiness depends on two
ingredients people don't think about: *God's word* and *obedience
to it*. Let's think about these components of cheerfulness.

ഗ്രൻ

What do you think makes most people happy?

As we've said, most people are made happy by their
families, at least that's a common belief. When the kids get a
sound education, locate a dependable job, or rise higher in
the company where they work, Mom and Dad are exuberant.
I know, because I often hear what church members' children
accomplish, and I'm glad to be informed. Then I can rejoice
with the family. Besides, church friends also have to listen

while I brag a bit! What good parent isn't thrilled to see children do well in life or find a virtuous spouse or present another generation of delightful children to be loved?

The woman who spoke to Jesus enjoyed the thought of his mother being happy to be his mother. During an encounter, she called out, "Blessed is the mother who gave you birth and nursed you" (Lk. 11:27). The word *blessed* means that someone's happy, but usually in the sense of being given God's favor or mercy. Blessed people consider themselves fortunate, although not in the sense of being lucky. To be blessed is to have good experiences, to receive God's caring concern, to walk a bit closer to the Almighty. This suggests that the woman who shouted to Jesus was herself a happy mother—with good, loving, successful children of her own—and she enjoyed the discovery of other joyful mothers. The imagined contentment of Mary as she nurtured Jesus brought enthusiasm to the woman's shouting voice.

A teacher was getting to know her students and asked one girl how many children were in her family. The girl answered, "Seven." The teacher suggested that having so many children in one family must cost a lot. "Oh, no," the girl answered. "We don't buy 'em. We just raise 'em."

It's been said that a truly happy person is the one whose children run into her arms when her hands are empty.

The woman's calling out to Jesus suggests that she was also a carefree religious person. Her heart sought after God. She attended Jesus' meeting and paid close attention to his lessons and stories. Jesus was a rabbi whose instruction brought her closer to God. The woman liked Jesus and was delighted to consider his family situation. Though she probably didn't know Mary, she called her blessed, just as Elizabeth had declared Jesus' mother to be fortunate. Surely, this fine teacher made his Mom happy! The woman knew that he made she herself joyful.

If you're not a parent, you may also be a happy religious person, with your heart earnestly seeking God. You might share this woman's excitement about Jesus' message, and it's a fine thing for you to do.

ଈୠ୰ଔ

Now consider this: What makes God's people truly happy?

As much as our kids and other people's productive children cause us to feel good and glad, this isn't the deepest satisfaction Jesus wants to bring into our lives. He had another standard of happiness. He said to the woman who was so enthusiastic about his mother: "Blessed rather are those who hear the word of God and obey it" (Lk. 11:21-28). His comment was in no way a put-down of Mary, nor a criticism of her faith in him nor of her joy at being his mother. Jesus' concern was the word of God.

To hear God's word requires patient listening. You have to spend time going over its thoughts. The time might be in the morning prior to starting your day or in the evening before retiring. A few people visit the scriptures twice a day. Regardless of when you meet God in his word, each day you must consider how the Lord's ideas impact your own. After understanding how you measure up against the Bible's teachings, you can assess your character and conduct better. After knowing what God expects his people to do, you can set about doing it. Jesus' concern was about the hearing of the Father's message. He was also concerned about people obeying God's word.

Why is it important for you to act on lessons you learn from the Bible? Because in scripture you find life's depth and breadth. Your personality's dimensions are enlarged when you live as God's word teaches. A tenacity develops in your heart so that you face hard times or cruel people with an understanding and a compassion uncommon among human beings. The Old and New Testaments are your God-given source of personal strength and wisdom. "The best measure of the spiritual life is not its ecstasies," Oswald Chambers said, "but its obedience." As you accomplish what Jesus teaches, you reveal God's power to sustain a life. You become a happy person who possesses joy broader than others possess, because you find it via in the Bible.

This emphasis on God's word rather than the usual sources of people's happiness wasn't because Jesus came from an unhappy family and looked for an outlet for his frustrations. Yes, he and his brothers were not always on the same page about his mission. Yes, his family worried about him. But by and large Jesus was a man from a happy family. He loved children and was concerned with how parents felt regarding his disciples' bad attitude. His love for others reveals his own family background, a home where children were cherished. He emphasized God's word because hidden within it is the power to confront life's difficulties with a joyful and hopeful attitude—one the strong man and the possessed person in Luke 11 could have used.

Jesus taught a clear, simple lesson to the woman who admired him and his mother. What's the lesson? *Happiness depends on two ingredients people don't think about: God's word and obedience to it.*

An old saying declares, "Satan isn't afraid of a Bible with dust on it." But he is afraid of one that's read, and more afraid of one that's obeyed. Shouldn't you begin, or continue, reading the Bible as a major source for your happy life?

You are witnesses, and so is God, of how holy, righteous and blameless we were among you who believed. For you know that we dealt with each of you as a father deals with his own children, encouraging, comforting and urging you to live lives worthy of God, who calls you into his kingdom and glory.

And we also thank God continually because, when you received the word of God, which you heard from us, you accepted it not as the word of men, but as it actually is, the word of God, which is at work in you who believe. For you, brothers, became imitators of God's churches in Judea, which are in Christ Jesus: You suffered from your own countrymen the same things those churches suffered from the Jews, who killed the Lord Jesus and the prophets and also drove us out. They displease God and are hostile to all men in their effort to keep us from speaking to the Gentiles so that they may be saved. In this way they always heap up their sins to the limit. The wrath of God has come upon them at last.

1 Thessalonians 2:10-16

3

THE WORD AT WORK

> And we also thank God continually because, when you received the word of God, which you heard from us, you accepted it not as the word of men, but as it actually is, the word of God, which is at work in you who believe.
>
> 1 Thessalonians 2:13

I don't know how true it is, but the story goes that when actor W. C. Fields, who was an agnostic, was on his deathbed, someone discovered him reading a Bible and asked him why he did so. Fields answered, "I'm looking for a loophole!"

Isn't this how many people use the scriptures? They think God's word, like most religious objects, is something for the end of life. Yet the Lord's word is at work in anyone who'll accept its message. What sort of labor does it do? Let's see.

കൗ

God's word works to give people gratitude. Isn't this one of the main reasons behind the Book of Psalms? People were moved to express thanks because God rescued them from trouble, or because they were thinking about his trustworthy character. The gospels show us people who praise God such as the mother whose son was raised from the dead at Nain or the blind man who saw for the first time in his life. Old Testament people and those from the New Testament era heard about God's grace available to them and rejoiced. They gave thanks because of what God's word taught them.

Paul told the Thessalonians he and his co-workers thanked the Lord because the believers at Thessalonica had received God's message *as God's word*. They listened to it as Paul, Silas and Timothy proclaimed it; they thought about it, discussed it and concluded it was, indeed, God's message. So they believed it. They accepted Jesus as God's Son, their Savior and Lord, and they acted faithfully on the principles Paul taught about him. Since the Thessalonians accepted Christ by receiving God's word *as his word*, they—like Paul—were grateful to the Lord for it. The word was at work in them. Thanks be to God!

How are people today made grateful by the Bible? An anonymous Christian answered this question well. "Christ is its grand subject," he wrote. "Our good is its design, and God's glory is its goal."

Have you discovered Jesus through reading the Bible? Have you had a better life because of learning his parables or applying the Sermon on the Mount to your conduct? Have you glimpsed the Lord's glory in the pages of the Bible? Then where's your gratitude? Why aren't you excited to read more about God's activity?

Consider how the Lord's word is at work in you, and tell him how you're thankful.

🕲🢒

God's word works because it isn't a merely human word. It's definite that the Bible was written in the languages of human beings—Aramaic, Hebrew and Greek. It's been translated to other human languages—Sahidic, Latin and English. The Bible tells stories about people, stories remembered from times when people lived in wandering tribal societies, stories from great empires, stories of ordinary people, tales of kings and heroes. The scriptures form a book about people, for people, and by people. Prophets wrote down their visions, poets penned their flowery words, and historians recorded the events behind the Exodus, the Exile, and the Church. God's word was written by people, yet it has a power of persuasion beyond merely human words. It consoles, corrects, and counsels. It rings loudly with a divine sound, with thoughts from the Almighty.

Paul explained to the Thessalonians. When they responded to God's word as he, Timothy and Silas preached it, they took it not as a human word, but as it actually is—the word of God. The Thessalonians could have considered the messages they heard to be simply human thinking about God, but they heard more in the sermons than plain words. The Lord's voice resonated inside them, and they believed what God said. They accepted Jesus as Savior. God's word worked in their hearts and minds because it wasn't entirely a human word. God's Spirit spoke through it.

About Bible reading, Puritan leader John Bunyan said, "Pray and read, read and pray; for a little from God is better than a great deal from men."

In school, you studied the writings of philosophers, scientists, mathematicians, economists, story writers. As great as Shakespearean literature is, it's influence is fading after a few centuries, but the Bible still sells more copies per year than any other single book. Why? Because its voice isn't an earthling's voice. Heaven speaks in scripture. God's word works because it isn't a merely human word.

೫ CR

Though it may seem repetitive, it needs to be said again: God's word works because it is *God's* word. As his message to humans, scripture is filled with the Father's advice. By it, he comforts the downhearted, cautions the hasty, and invigorates the weary. On the Bible's pages a message of hope spreads wide: *God loves you in his Son Jesus Christ*. Over and again, scripture repeats itself. It tells you what God wants you to hear. It's *his* word.

Paul told his friends in Thessalonica: "And we also thank God continually because, when you received the word of God, which you heard from us, you accepted it not as the word of men, but as it actually is, the word of God, which is at work in you who believe" (1 Th. 2:13).

If people accept it for what it is, the Bible defends itself as God's word. It convinces the skeptical mind; it unburdens the frazzled soul. Thessalonian Christians came into contact with the God who loved them in Jesus his Son. They were comforted, guided, given peace, grace. God's word worked within them because it is *God's* word, the message of the Almighty.

"Who speaks for God?" Charles Colson asked. "He does quite nicely for himself," Colson answered. "Through his holy and infallible word, and the quiet obedience of his servants."

Some people think if you ever get around to reading the whole Bible from Genesis to Revelation only one time in your life, you've done enough. But how can you be in contact with your Savior and hear what he wants you to do by only seldom studying the holy books that define his character and reveal his will? You must read the word of God through and through and through. Once isn't enough if you hope to find God's word at work in your life.

Start a daily practice of reading the Bible for your soul's sake. Don't wait until the beginning of next year. Dig into it. Start today. Your personal acquaintance with Jesus Christ will develop and flourish as you take his word into your heart and mind more each day.

For the word of God is living and active. Sharper than any double-edged sword, it penetrates even to dividing soul and spirit, joints and marrow; it judges the thoughts and attitudes of the heart. Nothing in all creation is hidden from God's sight. Everything is uncovered and laid bare before the eyes of him to whom we must give account.

Therefore, since we have a great high priest who has gone through the heavens, Jesus the Son of God, let us hold firmly to the faith we profess. For we do not have a high priest who is unable to sympathize with our weaknesses, but we have one who has been tempted in every way, just as we are—yet was without sin. Let us then approach the throne of grace with confidence, so that we may receive mercy and find grace to help us in our time of need.

Hebrews 4:12-16

4

THE ACTIVE WORD

...the word of God is living and active. Sharper than any double-edged sword, it penetrates even to dividing soul and spirit, joints and marrow; it judges the thoughts and attitudes of the heart.

Hebrews 4:12

A mountain family received the new pastor for a visit. Before the pastor left, he asked if the family wanted him to read from the Bible. "Why, shur!" the mother said. "Rubin, go git the Big Book we always read from." Her son fetched back the Sears Roebuck catalogue!

Many people want to be known as well-versed in the Bible, but in truth, few read it. Why? Because God's word opens the darkest corners your life and enlightens them. It's his living, active word. So people hide from its influence. They don't want to be changed too much! By ignoring scripture they can avoid God's renovations to their characters.

Let's think one more time about the nature and use of God's word.

℮ℭ

The author of Hebrews wrote, "...the word of God is living and active." Jesus is called the Living Word of God by many Christians past and present. He represents God's message in physical form and makes undeniable its claim on human souls. The books of the Old and New Testaments do the same thing if a person bothers to apply their message to his life, which may be why few read the Bible every day. They don't want God's message in physical form, and they don't want its claim made undeniable in their hearts.

In the Old West, loggers stamped the ends of their logs before floating them downriver. The stamp told which lumberman owned the log. A preacher was distressed when he spotted his church members hauling logs from another mill out of the water, cutting off the stamped ends, and burning them. Then they sawed the other logger's wood into lumber to ship to market.

On Sunday, the preacher proclaimed to his flock the meaning of the text, "Thou shalt not steal." After worship, everyone flattered him about his fine sermon. On Monday, the preacher was saddened as he watched his members cut the ends off more logs. The next Sunday's sermon was on the topic, "Thou shalt not cut the ends off thy neighbor's logs!" Following worship, his flock ran him out of town!

It's easier to read the Bible than to apply its message to your daily behavior. You're dealing with a living, active word from God himself. You're also dealing with your own heart and mind, and many people resist anything that demands a change in their poorly learned behaviors. Human beings have an independent streak that keeps them from surrendering to God's revealed will.

Hebrews commented about scripture that it is "...sharper than any double-edged sword..." In other words, the Good Book cuts through a person's self-righteous defenses, and with ease it removes God's competition for your heart and mind. It seeks humble, receptive tenderness, a ready, interested intelligence. Jesus taught the way. Learn the content of scripture, and live in its kind and energetic manner! Give up your self-interest, and take up the Lord's concerns!

The author of Hebrews also wrote that God's word "...penetrates even to dividing soul and spirit, joints and marrow..." The author was explaining how no part of your character escapes from God's powerful message. When you read the Bible or hear a sermon based on scripture, it grasps your being and splits your life into its hidden components. The good you think and feel is separated from the bad you think and feel. Your ambitions and humility are made visible in their crudeness or their courtesy. The Bible is a penetrating book.

A preacher told his congregation, "Next week, I'm going to preach about the sin of lying. To prepare, I hope all of you will read Mark 17 this week." The following Sunday, he asked how many people had read Mark 17. Every hand went up except one. "Martha," he asked, "why didn't you read Mark 17?"

"Because Mark has only *sixteen* chapters," the old woman said.

The preacher smiled and said, "And now I'll begin my sermon against telling lies."

As Hebrews explained about God's word, "…it judges the thoughts and attitudes of the heart." You cannot escape the Bible's assessment of your soul. You may run from it now by failure to open the word or read it, but at the judgment you'll answer God's word directly. "Why were your thoughts far from me? Why was your attitude in opposition to my will?" Face your Judge now while he's willing to forgive, or face him later when he's angry. His active and living word is your evaluator. It tests and tries your soul.

‽‸›

During World War II, a GI was stationed in the Pacific. He met an islander who proudly showed him a Bible. "We live by God's word," the native said.

"Oh," the soldier answered, "we've given up all that stuff!"

The islander answered, "It's a good thing we haven't given it up, or you'd be a meal by now."

God's word grasps the deepest corners of your being and reconstructs your life. It's his living, active word. Read it daily, and let it work on your character.

*In the original edition the following quotations
about the Bible were sidebars.
They are reproduced here at the end of Book 2.*

What the Bible Says About Itself...

Jesus said, "You diligently study the Scriptures because you think that by them you possess eternal life. These are the Scriptures that testify about me, yet you refuse to come to me to have life." (John 5:39-40)

For everything that was written in the past was written to teach us, so that through endurance and the encouragement of the Scriptures we might have hope. (Romans 15:4)

If you really keep the royal law found in Scripture, "Love your neighbor as yourself," you are doing right. (James 2:8)

He [Paul] writes the same way in all his letters, speaking in them of these matters. His letters contain some things that are hard to understand, which ignorant and unstable people distort, as they do the other Scriptures, to their own destruction. (2 Peter 3:16)

What People Say about the Bible

To what greater inspiration and counsel can we turn than to the imperishable truth to be found in this treasure house, the Bible? (Queen Elizabeth II)

On becoming more acquainted with the word of the Bible, I began to understand so much more of what I had been taught, and of what I had learned about life and about the people in mine. (Duke Ellington)

The whole hope of human progress is suspended on the ever-growing influence of the Bible. (William Seward)

The Word of God well understood and religiously obeyed is the shortest route to spiritual perfection. And we must not select a few favorite passages to the exclusion of others. Nothing less than a whole Bible can make a whole Christian. (A. W. Tozer)

Unless we form the habit of going to the Bible in bright moments as well as in trouble, we cannot fully respond to its consolations because we lack equilibrium between light and darkness. (Helen Keller)

Fun Facts about the Bible

Did you know the Bible was written in three languages? Hebrew, Greek and Aramaic.

The apostle Paul wrote 13 letters to churches or individuals—more Bible books than anyone else.

Scripture contains many kinds of literature: history, prophecy, poetry, legend, biography, short stories, other genres. It's a *library* rather than a *book*.

Bible books didn't have pages or covers at first. They were written by hand in ink on scrolls which were rolled up after being read.

The Bible was written over a period of 1500 to 2000 years by an unknown number of writers, editors and copyists.

It tells about people all around the Mediterranean: Hebrews, Greeks, Egyptians, Romans, Amorites, Babylonians, and others.

BOOK THREE
SEVEN WAYS TO GET CLOSE TO GOD

The apostle Paul tells us a wonderful truth about ourselves, a truth many believers don't take to heart. He wrote to the Ephesians: "Praise be to the God and Father of our Lord Jesus Christ, who has blessed us in the heavenly realms with every spiritual blessing in Christ. For he chose us in him before the creation of the world to be holy and blameless in his sight. In love he predestined us to be adopted as his sons through Jesus Christ, in accordance with his pleasure and will—to the praise of his glorious grace, which he has freely given us in the One he loves" (Eph. 1:3-6).

God graciously gave Christ's people a gift that he hasn't granted to other human beings. This isn't a reason to gloat or feel superior to anyone else on Planet Earth, but a Christian's status as an adopted child of God brings him or her resources not possessed by other people. You can live close to God and receive his daily help!

As a disciple of Jesus Christ, you have access to God in ways other people don't. Are you using your advantage of knowing God in Jesus Christ as fully as he wants you to use it? Here are *seven ways to get close to God* and find the daily help you need in the rushed and bothered world.

1
Prayer

What's the purpose of Christian prayer? Paul told the Colossian believers what it is. "Devote yourselves to prayer, being watchful and thankful" (Col. 4:2). As you pray, you remain watchful—alert and on guard. You also remain thankful, grateful to God for the daily supply of your bread, the assistance he gives in time of crisis, the comfort he offers when worry or fear or sorrow threatens. The purpose of Christian prayer is to draw out of you a devoted dependence on God as you go about your life.

A convenient formula to follow when you pray will help focus your prayers and give you a sense of confidence as you pray. This formula will help you to avoid the "Gimmee" kind of prayer that seems to have become the standard form for many people: "Lord, give me this. Lord, give me that." Gimmee prayers treat God as a celestial Santa Claus! The formula is old, tried, and true. It's also simple: A. C. T. S. In other words, make your prayers start with *Adoration,* then add *Confession,* followed by *Thanksgiving,* and end with your *Supplications* (your Gimmees).

Here's a short example of a prayer offered according to the ACTS formula: "Lord God, I praise you for being my wonderful Savior, and I admit my sinfulness and my neglect of our relationship. Thank you for forgiving me because of Jesus' death on the cross. Help me to live a holier life. Also, guide my friend Sally as she makes a major decision. In Jesus' name, I ask you to accept my prayer. Amen."

Can you pick out each part of the prayer formula in the above example? Use it in most of your prayers, and it'll quickly become a habit that keeps your petitions on track and your heart open to God's influence and blessings.

Mark Twain pointed out another helpful hint about your prayer life. He once said, "It is best to read the weather forecasts before we pray for rain." I agree. We're too quick to pray for matters about which it's unnecessary to petition heaven.

Use your noggin when you're on your knees! It'll get you closer to God.

2
Bible Study

What's the purpose of the Bible? The apostle Paul explained to his coworker Timothy: "All Scripture is God-breathed and is useful for teaching, rebuking, correcting and training in righteousness, so that the man of God may be thoroughly equipped for every good work" (2 Tim. 3:16-17). The Bible is the Almighty's gift to his people, and it's designed by the Holy Spirit to be both a useful tool for living your life in this demanding world and a way to enter into an intimate conversation with the living God. The result of a consistent plan of personal Bible study is that you'll be prepared to do whatever tasks come your way, and you'll do them in a holy and faithful manner.

Have you ever wanted to know what God wants you to do? Have you wished you had confidence to try doing want you think he wants you to do? Then get into the scriptures on a daily basis. It's all in there! God doesn't re-invent the wheel! He explained centuries ago everything necessary for you to know. As you develop a daily habit of reading scripture, you'll find yourself getting into a closer fellowship with God all the time. His blessings come when his word is heard.

How can you do such a Bible study? This is what works for me: Pick a Bible book, read one chapter from it every day, thinking about its message and listening for whatever God's Spirit might be applying to my person or life. Carry on a conversation with the Lord about the chapter you're reading. When you finish that chapter, read the following chapter the next day. Keep the discussion going. When you finish that Bible book, pick another one, and keep reading a chapter a day. Some chapters may be long, but others will be brief. A nice balance will develop in your talks with the Master.

I also like to alternate back and forth from the Old Testament to the New Testament, but I sense sometimes that Christ Jesus wants me to read a particular book. So I go with it. He's the one who guides our discussions. Yet the habit of meeting him every day should be like meeting friends at the diner for morning coffee. You simply do it for the fun of the conversation!

About Bible study, Daniel Webster wrote, "I believe that the Bible is to be understood and received in the plain and obvious meaning of its passages, since I cannot persuade myself that a book intended for the instruction and conversion of the whole world, should cover its meaning in such mystery and doubt, that none but critics and philosophers can discover it."

In other words, if you feel ill-equipped to study the Bible, remember that God's word was written with you in mind. It isn't a specialized book that he reserves for scholars or other people who know Greek and Hebrew and have read a lot about the ancient world. The Bible is God's Word to *you*. He means for it to bring you closer to himself, but that will never happen as fully as he wants it to happen unless you start reading scripture and continue to read a bit of it every day.

3
Meditation

What's the purpose of Christian meditation? The apostle Paul wrote to the Philippians about this: "...whatever is true, whatever is noble, whatever is right, whatever is pure, whatever is lovely, whatever is admirable—if anything is excellent or praiseworthy—think about such things" (Phil. 4:8). When he created you, God gave you a head and a heart. He intends that you use both of them well. Fill your mind and your emotions with excellent thoughts and feelings. Don't think about lies and how to lie. Don't read about crass and base behavior. Christians should be careful about how much drivel and silliness they allow into their hearts. A mental diet of too many sitcoms from television will dull your appreciation of high ethical behavior. What goes into your brain and heart pops out in your behavior. This is why Paul wanted Christians to consider—to meditate—on admirable matters, excellence and praiseworthy deeds and attitudes. Just as the condition of your body in determined by what you feed it, so your spirit is shaped by what you think and feel!

So how can you meditate as a Christian? Begin by using a *focus phrase*. Sit in a comfortable chair. Turn off the music, even Christian music. Tune out every distraction in the house or on the street or in the hall. How? By repeating quietly or silently a phrase such as one of these:

"Lord Jesus Christ, have mercy on me a sinner."

"Holy Spirit, Comforter, still my heart."

"Father in heaven, send calmness into my soul."

Make up a short sentence of your own, or borrow one from a biblical book such as Proverbs. Repeat your focus phrase several times until you sense your head and heart aiming at God. Your goal is to be alone with the Almighty.

Now begin to *listen*. Has a thought come into your mind? Are you feeling an emotion? Where did it come from? God? Yourself? A bad impulse? The Lord Jesus is active through his Holy Spirit in your subconscious all the time, especially if you're in prayer frequently and if you read the scriptures often. Listen for an indication of something you need to think about or something you're bothered by. Allow thoughts and emotions to start flowing unhindered. When you feel as if your mind and heart are getting too busy to sort things out by yourself, say a short prayer. Ask the Holy Spirit to make things clear to you.

Now you're ready for a third step: *Writing*. Keep a diary or a journal. Start to record what you think and feel. Allow your sentences to be random if they want to be. Gradually, you'll sense an order developing. Re-write if you're led to do so. Get your emotions and insights down on paper where you can read them, sort them, discard or embellish them. Writing brings clarity to your meditations.

Be sure to ask yourself at some point during each time of meditation: *Where's God in all this?* Record what you understand about the Lord's part in your musings. Preserve your writings, and from time to time—months and years later—read them again. You'll be surprised at how dynamic your relationship with Christ has become through this exercise in meditative devotions.

"Devotion," Douglas Steere wrote in *Prayer and Worship*, "is not a thing which passes, which comes and goes, as it were, but it is something habitual, fixed, permanent, which extends over every instant of life and regulates all our conduct."

Such meditation also brings you consciously closer to God.

4
Worship

What's the purpose of Christian worship? To the Roman believers, Paul said, "...I urge you...in view of God's mercy, to offer your bodies as living sacrifices, holy and pleasing to God—this is your spiritual act of worship" (Rom. 12:1). The word *spiritual* can also be translated as *reasonable*. So many people think worship is a matter of feelings, an emotional contact with the divine. It's also a matter of intellectual contact with the divine. When you worship God, your whole being—body and soul—is involved with the heavenly One who has been so good and generous with you. In Jesus Christ, God rescued you from sin and death and placed you into a living relationship with himself. It is both reasonable and spiritual for you to surrender your entire person to a lifestyle that rejoices in your Savior and expresses the value you place on him. In other words, your closeness to God is expressed in your worship of him.

Now worship has two dimensions: a *corporate* and a *private* measurement. You gather together with other believers at a given time and place and engage in a liturgy, a series of worshipful activities. You sing, pray, contribute money, read scripture, listen to the word expounded, and express your sense of how marvelous God is, and you do this in the company of other Christians. Worship is a corporate experience.

It is also a private experience. Public worship has a personal side. You'll get out of a service at any given place or time only what you privately put into it. Nod off, and what good has your attendance achieved? You have to be consciously part of a worship event to benefit from it. Yet there's a wider sense to your private worship. When you notice God's handiwork in a snowflake, that's private worship, especially if you say, "You're a good Creator,

Lord!" Private worship occurs whenever you know you're in the presence of your Redeemer and acknowledge his presence with gratitude. You could be sitting at a stoplight and observe a kind act on the sidewalk, and your heart says, "Blessed Lord, it's good to see how you're getting through to earth's people." How well do you take brief moments to enjoy God? Such private worship, like corporate worship, will draw you closer to the One you praise.

Thomas Carlyle wrote, "The man who does not habitually worship is but a pair of spectacles behind which there is no eye."

Make worship so habitual in your daily routine that you learn to see the Creator, the Savior or the Advocate in your home, on your job, among your friends, and even on a street full of strangers. Such a worshipful attitude makes you aware of the God who never leaves or forsakes you, who's always close at hand.

5
Communion

What's the purpose of communion? The apostle Paul wrote to the Corinthian church: "…whenever you eat this bread and drink this cup, you proclaim the Lord's death until he comes" (1 Cor. 11:26). This, of course, speaks about the sacrament of the Lord's supper, communion. The sacrament is a means for God to get his grace into his people's lives in an active way. As you share bread and wine, praying with Christ's gathered people and considering the significance of what the church does in this ritual, you sense the other participant in the rite, God himself. The whole Trinity is there—Father, Son and Holy Spirit. Within a congregation, fellowship with God around the sacred table creates a knowledge of his love and presence. We draw close to him, and he to us.

Within an individual Christian, new knowledge of Jesus the Christ develops, too. As you partake of the bread, you discern the broken body of your Savior. As you drink the wine, you remember his sacrifice. You sense how awesome has been his commitment to you, and you walk a little closer to your Lord. You also know that he's with you.

Richard Raines explained the nature of the Christian community. He said, "Christianity is like electricity. It cannot enter a person unless it can pass through." During a communion service, it's often the "passing through" of the Holy Spirit's vigor that impresses Christians. We feel the divine close at hand. We enjoy our Lord and glorify him by praise and fellowship on a high spiritual level.

6
Fellowship

What's the purpose of Christian fellowship? It can be understood when you consider what Paul said about his first trip to Jerusalem after becoming a Christian. On that trip he met some of the original disciples. "James, Peter and John, those reputed to be pillars," Paul reported, "gave me and Barnabas the right hand of fellowship when they recognized the grace given to me. They agreed that we should go to the Gentiles, and they to the Jews" (Gal. 2:9).

Prior to his conversion, Paul persecuted the church violently, but once the church's leaders were convinced about the reality of his conversion, they accepted him into the ranks of the apostles. He, too, was a person called to serve Jesus Christ for the salvation of others. James, Peter and John—the inner circle of Jesus' original disciples—welcomed Paul into their fellowship. The purpose of Christian fellowship is to bless Christian people with one another's company as they all serve Jesus together. Each of us needs to know we aren't alone in the call to proclaim the gospel. Fellowship provides the support and encouragement we need.

Christian life is lived in a corporate (bodily) setting. As one believer joins others in the walk of faith, each one grows in grace and vigor. In the process of fellowship, Christians are brought closer to God by having the comfort and support of other members of Christ's body.

An unknown but wise believer said, "The church is never a place, but always a people. It's never a fold but always a flock, never a stately building but always a believing community. The church is you who pray, not a place where you pray." By knowing one another well, each one is drawn closer to the Lord we serve together.

7
Service

What's the purpose of Christian service? Paul also explained this important piece of coming closer to God. He told the Corinthians, "Because of the service by which you have proved yourselves, men will praise God for the obedience that accompanies your confession of the gospel of Christ, and for your generosity in sharing with them and with everyone else" (2 Cor. 9:13).

Serving the needs of others both inside and outside the church, a Christian is drawn into a life of obedience and of unity with others whom God touches with his grace. Finding ways to help "the least and the lost," you discover yourself accompanied by the God whom you serve. In Matthew 25, Jesus himself explained a truth of Christian living: "Doing something for one of the least of these is doing something for me." In the people you serve, you discover your living God.

An Irish proverb reminds us: "God likes people when he helps people."

When you also help them in Jesus' name, you find yourself growing to like the people you help. Your greatest blessing comes when you one day see with clarity that those you help are revealing to you the very closeness God grants to us all.

No one of these ways of drawing close to God is sufficient by itself alone. All of them must be combined into the fabric of your life for you to know every day the presence and guidance of God through Jesus Christ and his Holy Spirit. The challenge of Christian living begins in the acceptance of your Lord's established disciplines for growth. It continues in the practice of those principles which Christians across the millennia have found useful and beneficial.

Have you been using the seven tools to move closer to God? Perhaps you haven't been putting all of them to work. Pinpoint which ones you should work on. Find a friend who'll help you, maybe a pastor, a Bible study leader, or an acquaintance at church who seems to be spiritually mature. Ask someone you trust to talk with you about your progress in the chosen disciplines during the next month or two. See where God leads you. If nothing else, you ought to get closer to him!

BOOK 4
CENTERED LIVING

God's Enemy in the Human Heart

After this I had been telling him how the devil was God's enemy in the hearts of men, and used all his malice and skill to defeat the good designs of Providence, and to ruin the kingdom of Christ in the world, and the like. "Well," says Friday, "but you say God is so strong, so great; is He not much strong, much might as the devil?" "Yes, yes," says I, "Friday, God is stronger than the devil; God is above the devil, and therefore we pray to God to tread him down under our feet, and enable us to resist his temptations, and quench his fiery darts." "But," says he again, "if God much strong, much might as the devil, why God no kill the devil, so make him no more do wicked?"

Daniel Defoe, *Robinson Crusoe*

Introduction

Surely, you've observed an acquaintance, a co-worker, or someone close to you as he began a promising life. Then a few years later, you watched in confusion as the life came apart. Your college buddy was intelligent. Endowed with internal qualities that made him popular, he seemed to be an ensured success. He started his chosen career, which suited him well. You noted his excitement. People felt he'd reach a high position and receive a respected reputation. Future employers would seek out his skills and pay well for them. Colleagues would try to follow in his footsteps. You don't know what happened, but your friend changed. His interests shifted and re-shifted until he took up an unrelated career, then one more. His life spiraled away from his younger dreams. He moved toward no particular goal. He drifted. The spiral twisted downward, and when you met him years afterward, you encountered a caustic fellow.

Why do talented people with natural instincts, who are eager to achieve big dreams, self-destruct? Why do they unhinge themselves from their once stubbornly claimed goals? Why do they dissolve into a shadow of what they promised to become? Is there a clue, a secret to avoid, a way to spot disaster in the making? If there is a telltale sign that might warn *you* to beware a similar fate, wouldn't you heed the alarm?

This book, *Centered Living*, describes a major cause for people starting well in life but ending poorly. The intent of it is to help you think through a crucial area of your Christian living, indeed, of all humans' conduct. If people understood what lies at the center of genuinely Christian behavior, their lives would have the focus all of us need in order to experience life as it's intended to be practiced. Understanding how to avoid a primary pitfall behind self-deterioration would afford all of us a valuable opportunity to become what we were created to be. The book is about how to give your life the focus it needs.

God intends for you to live abundantly, and he sent Jesus of Nazareth, along with other instructors, to teach the way to find it. There's a wellspring from which flows the meaning and excitement we crave in our lives. The energy that emerges from people who discover the core of Christian discipleship improves how they act and how they produce a happier world.

The promise of a centered lifestyle is that you receive strength, courage, and the skill to shine throughout your days on earth.

Larry Armstrong

Chapter 1
Life's Wellspring

In today's world, when you speak about guarding your heart, you're probably thinking how to insulate yourself against the hurt of a lost love. A jewelry commercial picks up on this thought and has an actress explain how her mother used to tell her: "Keep your heart open, and love will always find a way."

A common misbelief in our society is that an open heart gives you a greater opportunity to experience life's wonder and its joys. To an extent, this is true, but is it not also a falsehood? Opening your heart to any teasing influence can entice you to disaster. You need guidance on how to weigh what appeals to your heart, especially if you're going to be a faithful disciple of Jesus Christ.

The biblical book of Proverbs offers you such practical assistance. "Above all else, guard your heart," the Bible says, "for it is the wellspring of life" (Prov. 4:23). *Above all else, guard your heart.* Protect what goes into your soul, because opening yourself to all things isn't the way to experience full human integrity. Why? Because your heart is the source of both your good and bad practices. An unguarded heart quickly loses its reliability. Consider how the biblical proverb applies to your daily living.

Good Advice

A wise Old Testament instructor offered students good advice. In fact, he spoke like a father, when he instructed his readers.

My son, pay attention to what I say;
    listen closely to my words.
Do not let them out of your sight,
    keep them within your heart;
for they are life to those who find them
    and health to a man's whole body.

Proverbs 4:20-22

The author of Proverbs was a sage who instructed Israel's people in prudent conduct and sensible attitudes that produced wholesome character. He encouraged readers to pay close attention, to perk up their ears, and take heed. His lessons should be kept in people's hearts. Memorize what he had to say—that was his sound advice. Why? Because his shrewd counsel would mean life to those who understood it. Even a physically healthy body should result from carefully following the biblical philosopher's instruction.

If I had only listened to the knowledgeable advice of my physical education and health teachers when I was in high school and college, maybe I wouldn't be fighting the weight battle as an aging man. I'm sure some of my mistakes could've been avoided had I heeded my parents' advice when I lived at home, and even afterward. Friends have given well-meaning warnings over the years, and I should have sometimes listened to them more closely. I'd have saved myself wasted effort and much frustration.

God's word offers those who read it sound direction, too. I can testify that when a person listens to the precepts laid down in scripture, life goes better. The good advice in the Bible is the heavenly Father's instruction that we ought to paste in front of our eyes. We ought to bury this treasure in the field of our hearts, so that we can dig it up as we need wisdom. The Bible contains life for those who mine its riches. It brings health even to their bodies.

The Church of Scotland sent its first missionary to India in 1829, Alexander Duff. He packed along with him a personal library of nearly 800 books. On the voyage, his ship was wrecked on a reef just miles from the coast of India.

Clinging to part of the hull throughout the night, he and other passengers were rescued in the morning, but their belongings were lost. As Duff stood onshore, he looked wistfully across the blue water, wondering how he'd teach, having lost his whole library. Then he spied a small box floating toward land. He retrieved it, and inside was his Bible! This would be his entire resource. At once, he led the survivors in a reading of Psalm 107, which is often called the traveler's psalm.

Over the following months, Duff taught five young people in the open air under a tree, using only the text of his precious Bible. His class grew to be more than 300 individuals, and from it sprang a school which provided the fledgling mission church of India with its educated leaders and preachers.

Billy Graham has often called on people to heed God's word. "May we store up the truths of God's word as much as possible," he said.

The Lord's advice in scripture is a source of life in your soul. Are you listening to his voice as he instructs you? A daily habit of reading through the Bible will do more to guard your heart than you might imagine, since the habit creates the protective content of your inner being. When trouble or temptation sneaks up and hits the back of your head, you'll recover more quickly because you'll have the ballast of God's own wisdom to maintain your poise and stability. The Lord's advice is always useful because of what it accomplishes. It begins to focus your life.

A Good Heart

A good heart is always your best goal. Whether you're a church officer or a pastor or an average member, the content of your heart will mean life for the church where you worship. Are you a doctor, a teacher in public school or in Sunday school? Are you a factory worker, a retired volunteer in a community group, or a homemaker? No matter what you do—

Above all else, guard your heart,
for it is the wellspring of life.

Proverbs 4:23

What happens in a church, on the job, among colleagues, and in your home is colored or cancelled out by the content of your heart. Fill yourself with deep sorrow or bitterness, and you'll create grief and resentment in those around you. O how important your heart's content is! What's inside you destroys or builds up those of us who encounter you. What an awesome responsibility! You can improve or destroy anyone's day with a word. And Christ means to call upon you to account for how you applied within your relationships what he's put into your soul.

I think the apostle Paul understood the importance of the human heart. As he wrote to friends in the ancient church at Philippi: "...whatever is true, whatever is noble, whatever is right, whatever is pure, whatever is lovely, whatever is admirable—if anything is excellent or praiseworthy—think about such things. Whatever you have learned or received or heard from me, or seen in me—put it into practice. And the God of peace will be with you" (Phil. 4:8).

Life goes better when your heart is full of virtue. Paul lived this truth, and he encouraged others to imitate him. Why? Because this lifestyle provides the focus you need.

More than anything else you do in your day-to-day activities, protect your heart! Put good things into it, and keep those attributes safe and sharp. Draw on your heart's store of high-quality traits, and make today better than yesterday. Your heart is the wellspring of your life and the lives of people near you. It's the deep, cool, refreshing source from which you draw living water, unless you allow it to be contaminated by cruel words or spite or meanness or unkind thoughts. Guard your heart, because it's the wellspring of your life, and what comes from it alters other people's experiences.

As the apostle James asked, "Can both fresh water and saltwater flow from the same spring?" (Jas. 3:11) Christian disciples must be consist sources of fresh water, the water of life, or what they spew out will harm rather than refresh.

Always recall the old computer programmer's warning: *GIGO!* "Garbage In, Garbage Out!"

Explaining one of his parables to Peter, Jesus said, "…the things that come out of the mouth come from the heart, and these make a man 'unclean.' For out of the heart come evil thoughts, murder, adultery, sexual immorality, theft, false testimony, slander" (Mt. 15:18). Wasn't Jesus encouraging the disciple to guard his heart because it was the wellspring of his life?

Shouldn't you and I also work toward having a well-centered heart? useful thoughts? virtuous feelings? The reason there are adulterers is that someone lusted for pleasures that don't belong to them as married people. The reason someone is murdered has to do with the ingredients that make up the disheveled mind of the murderer. Satan may be God's enemy in the human heart, as Robinson Crusoe believed, but we assist the adversary if we aren't vigilant. An evil thought produces evil deeds. Shouldn't you and I fill ourselves with virtuous ideas and useful knowledge, with decent emotions and first-rate imaginings?

A good heart is always your best goal, because it brings the focus you need.

Good Conduct

Consider another truth: A good conduct flows from your guarded heart. As the book of Proverbs instructed its readers…

> Let your eyes look straight ahead,
>   fix your gaze directly before you.
> Make level paths for your feet
>   and take only ways that are firm.
> Do not swerve to the right or the left;
>   keep your foot from evil.

Proverbs 4:24-27

How can you protect your heart? Look straight ahead. Learn what's noble, wholesome, pure and honest. Then keep your eyes fixed forward. Paths you walk as a church or civic leader, as a business person or a housewife are full of slippery spots and rough terrain. Look where you put your feet! Make sure of the footing before you step. Stride on solid ground not slick stones. Stay on the path! If you swerve left or right, you'll go down! "Keep your foot from evil." That's how to protect your soul's content. Put good stuff into it, and your walk is steady and healthy.

The Lord Jesus also taught this idea. In the Sermon on the Mount, he said, "…small is the gate and narrow the road that leads to life, and only a few find it" (Mt. 7:14).

In his poem, *A Psalm of Life*, Henry Wadsworth Longfellow advised his readers:

> Trust no future, howe'er pleasant!
> Let the dead past bury its dead!
> Act—act in the living Present!
> Heart within and God o'erhead!

I find this to be good advice. If your heart is full of quality feelings and thoughts, if you know God is with you, then you can abandon yourself to the day, and to the people who share it with you. Whether the future brings good or ill matters little. The mistakes of the past are gone. You're free to enjoy, released to live, permitted to venture about the earth with hope and intent. You can move forward in life, because the content of your soul is worth using, valuable enough to share.

But this adventure is a narrow road. The requirement to fill your heart with good things is a demanding task. You must select between choices that appear on the surface equally useful. You have to exercise a rigorous discernment, and that's beyond a human's natural ability to do consistently day after day. You come back again to the need for washing your soul in the word of God. He has spoken in scripture the wisdom you need. Having soaked yourself in its truths, you'll have a plentiful store of assets to put to work.

Still, the effort restrains you, since you cannot make a choice willy-nilly, without regard for compassion toward others and for truth in your dealings. You must find the narrow road, and stay on it. Yet this is made hazardous by the competing items in your heart—vices, wickedness, and impiety along with integrity and honor. So confession may be in order. Express to the Lord Jesus the sorrow you feel at being less than full of heart with his teachings. The natural inclination of the human heart is to fill itself with the pleasures of a moment rather than the treasures of eternity. So repentance is necessary. You have to proceed with the filling of your heart, then empty out some of its less usable contents, and re-fill it with better stuff, smarter wisdom. The road is narrow, and you must retreat often into God's word with his Spirit as your guide. You have to ask how scripture's truth modifies your behavior. Then you can be filled and filled again with the wisdom you seek.

Republican presidential candidate Barry Goldwater's 1964 campaign slogan was "In your heart you know he's right." Since the Arizona senator lost the election, we can guess that not everyone's heart agreed with him. Yet such an outcome does prove what the Bible says: The content of your heart controls what you do. It's the center of life. With it you choose your directions in an election and in life as a whole.

Heed the proverb's injunction: *Above all else, guard your heart.* Why? Because your heart is life's wellspring. What you put in it determines what comes out! Make sure your heart is aimed toward Christ Jesus. Behave as he teaches you to behave, and an abundant life bubbles up within and around you.

Chapter 2
An Abundant Heart

At Christmastime every year, we hear about love, peace and joy. Hope is all around. After the holidays end, snow settles over the land, frigid air keeps us indoors, and we're separated from others. Because of the darkened season, sour moods pervade our homes, and pessimism blankets human hearts during the winter months.

Yet cynicism and the distrust it breeds aren't reserved for the cold times. Gloom shades the human heart at any moment, often unexpectedly. The sunshine of May ought to lift your spirit, but an unexplainable wraith hovers over you. You feel silhouetted, covered by a dimness that saps your energy. Without warning you're plunged into a depressed state. Misery, despair and sadness pervade. Pessimism is always a danger skulking around the human soul.

Let's take a look at one of the Bible's curmudgeons. You know, an ill-tempered, crusty old guy who seems to have a vinegary outlook on life but speaks sensibly about how we feel. The author of Ecclesiastes appears to have been an embittered pessimist. He said things like this: "The hearts of men…are full of evil and there is madness in their hearts while they live, and afterward they join the dead" (Eccl. 9:3b). It sounds as though he genuinely believed everybody has evil in their hearts, and death is all we can expect. What a gloomy Gus!

But he could be onto something important. Let's see if we can get help from him for managing our blues. Can he teach us how to control our negativity?

What lies ahead?

First, he addressed the question: What lies ahead? Then he answered: *Nobody knows what lies ahead*. His own words were clear, "...I reflected on all this and concluded that the righteous and the wise and what they do are in God's hands, but no man knows whether love or hate awaits him" (Eccl. 9:1).

All people wish they knew what was coming their direction. Will others care about them or despise them? Is God on their side or not? That's the form this question takes when a person faces cancer or a loss of employment or falls down the apartment stairs. After he reflected on life's difficulties, the author of Ecclesiastes concluded that nobody knows what lies on the path ahead. You could be among God's favored folks, or you might be a person he judges to be insufficient. Life might be on the upswing for you— prosperity, security, good health—yet there's indication the Lord is unhappy with you. There's no way to tell, the author concludes. Everyone "shares a common destiny." Righteous or wicked, it doesn't matter. Decent, indecent, faithful at the temple or not, your individual character is insignificant. You could be sincerely pious or you might be outrageously impious... everybody comes to the same end. He probably means death. He definitely means you do not know what is around the next bend on your life's journey. God will do with you as God chooses.

This sentiment lies behind an assertion preachers hear regularly: "We all worship the same God. We're all going to the same place. We're just getting there from different directions." How nearsighted! How opposed to what the Lord himself says elsewhere in scripture!

The disciple Thomas said to Jesus, "Lord, we don't know where you are going, so how can we know the way?" Then the Lord answered, "I am the way and the truth and the life. No one comes to the Father except through me" (Jn. 14:5-6).

In a sense, everybody shares a common fate, but nobody knows what lies ahead. Whether new neighbors will like you or cheat you, tolerate you or hate you, nobody can say. No one can announce for certain that God will rescue you. Only you can sense the truth in your heart, and even *you* cannot declare your salvation with absolute conviction. You can only say, "I believe Jesus is the way to God, and I trust him to take me to the heavenly Father someday." Yet you don't know what lies ahead, not really. You can only believe what you're taught, what you believe or assume. Scripture says, "Now faith is being sure of what we hope for and certain of what we do not see" (Heb. 11:1).

C. S. Lewis explained how we should approach the future. "The next moment is as much beyond our grasp, and as much in God's care, as that a hundred years away," he said. "Care for the next minute is as foolish as care for a day in the next thousand years. In neither can we do anything, in both God is doing everything."

Dare you insist that you know what's coming? If you follow Jesus Christ, be careful how you answer. Many unthinking people claim that they can see what's about to hit them, and by intuition they're sometimes right. More often than not, they're inaccurate. Reliance on God is the best approach, trust without worry over what might happen. A disciple's task is to be certain of what cannot be seen—that is, to live each day by faith in the Lord and by obedience to him. With Christ as your focal point, what lies ahead is less important than what you're doing for him now.

How does it end?

Second, the author of Ecclesiastes addressed another question: How does it end? Then he answered: *Everybody comes to the same end.* In his own words, he elaborated,

This is the evil in everything that happens under the sun: The same destiny overtakes all. The hearts of men, moreover, are full of evil and there is madness in their hearts while they live, and afterward they join the dead (Eccl. 9:3).

Death…that's the common end of all living creatures. From the snail to the fish to the dog to the ape to the human being, death trails every breathing thing. All plants die eventually, including the giant redwoods that have lived for millennia. This biblical curmudgeon from Ecclesiastes announced what we all know and don't want to face. He demanded that his readers cope with their deaths, not because he was an incurable pessimist, but because he was a realist. Everybody dies. So don't run from it! Admit the truth! Then deal with it!

He confessed the reason why the same destiny assails us all. Our human hearts are full of evil and madness. Think about it. How many times have you been a foolish person, out of your right mind? Come now. You decided to do something foolhardy, dangerous, imprudent. I did. I went swimming in a quarry that was more than sixty feet deep and full of cold water in August. My friends and I weren't supposed to be there, but nobody could see us. We took an awful chance. It's a good thing none of us teenagers were discovered. It's better yet that none of us drowned! All people of whatever age do things that don't come from sound minds, but from foolish thinking.

Our human hearts are full of madness. And sin is just as prevalent as our foolishness. It's part of the reason all of us die at some point in time. The lowliest microbe, the elegantly designed human being are both destined to expire. You cannot ignore the fact forever, although you may have plastic surgery, buy tons of cosmetics, and work out 30 minutes three times each week in an attempt to stay young or healthy. Death is a specified reality in a world that was warped long ago by the sinful choices of our souls.

War is caused, always, by the content of human hearts. People fear or hate or cheat or do any number of deeds inspired by the interior of their souls, and war occurs. What's the cost? From 1914 to 1918, the years of World War I, 53 million men wore the uniforms of soldiers and sailors. Close to 13 million died in battle. Other casualties swelled the losses to 37 million. The manifold lusts in human hearts robbed the world of creative, energetic people, perhaps one who would have discovered the cure for cancer or brought us inventions to make life more enjoyable. Sin permits death to raise its ugly head, and it destroys so much more than we realize.

The human heart could be an abundant heart, full of treasure. Often it is, but from its scarcity, death also creeps prematurely into the world. What's inside us isn't always good. We don't debate this. We admit the truth about ourselves, or at least about those less productive folks over there. The wicked content of the interior human life devastates too much!

Here's a rock-solid reason for you to guard your heart above all else. You won't keep from dying in due time, but you'll live more intelligently and productively until you do. Protect your heart by putting into it only the best thoughts and feelings; then an abundant heart can be yours. When you reach our common destiny, your life will have counted as one well lived, as a bountiful gift. You don't have to self-destruct! You can end better than you started! Keep your focus on Jesus, and centered living will guide you to the right end.

Which is better?

Third, the author of Ecclesiastes tackled the question: Which is better? Then he answered: *Life is better than death.* It sounds as if he quoted a proverbial statement: "Anyone who is among the living has hope—even a live dog is better off than a dead lion!" (Eccl. 9:4) What a neat image! Dogs in the ancient world were usually seen as dirty, wild and worthless. Yes, people had little pet dogs, and huge guard dogs, but the average mongrel was looked down on. Yet an old saying declared that a living dog was better off than a dead lion. Don't you agree? The king of beasts might have been a ferocious and fearful opponent, but once slain, it was no longer a threat. Any dog who killed it was better off!

Life is better than death! If you're alive, you at least know that some-day you'll be dead. So what you choose to do now will make your living days either better or worse. So choose to live happily! Determine to a useful person and to relish the comforts you receive, because God's being good to you. As the author of Ecclesiastes put it, "Go, eat your food with gladness, and drink your wine with a joyful heart, for it is now that God favors what you do. Always be clothed in white, and always anoint your head with oil. Enjoy life with your wife, whom you love, all the days of this meaningless life that God has given you under the sun—all your meaningless days. For this is your lot in life and in your toilsome labor under the sun" (Eccl. 9:7-9).

The curmudgeon was a realist more than a pessimist, but he had a point. Life is better than death! Yet the poor fellow missed the good news of the gospel. As Jesus explained, "The thief comes only to steal and kill and destroy; I have come that they may have life, and have it to the full" (Jn. 10:10). The Lord's intention is that you live abundantly.

Some Christians are afraid to enjoy good things in life. They feel guilty because they can afford a fine home and dependable car. I've talked with faithful church members who think they ought to give up what God has settled into their laps. "After all," they reason, "Jesus owned no place to lay his head, so why am I favored with such a good situation?" My answer is, "Because God has things he wants you to do with your wealth. He wishes you'd give a fair amount to feed the hungry and clothe the naked. But he also hopes you take your spouse to dinner and relax together. He wants you to educate your kids and to be happy where you live and work. Focus less on money, more on opportunities to serve others. Rejoice in God's goodness, and to get closer to Christ."

God knows that life in a fractured world isn't easy. Sin creates havoc and restrains holiness. It's possible to be depressed and think life is awful, but the Lord has made your time a wondrous experience, too! He expects you to put your head up, look around at the delights he sets before you. Take pleasure in your spouse and learn how to genuinely like your children. Don't just love them, discover how to *like* them, to be fond of the way they smile, to dote on their accomplishments. Be as happy as God wants you to be! He gives you the tools and chances to use them daily. Build a life worthy of him. Don't stew over what you can't change. Make Jesus the hub of your life; then stretch yourself to become all he wants you to be. Live abundantly!

The author of Ecclesiastes wasn't entirely wrong. His words spoke a partial truth when he said, "The hearts of men...are full of evil and there is madness in their hearts while they live, and afterward they join the dead" (Eccl. 9:3*b*). It sounds as if he believed all people have evil in their hearts, and death is all we can expect. In a sense, it's true. All people fall short of God's image, in which he created them to exist, and the penalty for the heinous choice is death. Yet this is only half the truth.

The Christian gospel also declares that all people have evil in their hearts. Yet death isn't the end. We're steeped in sin. Bad attitudes leech out of us to become a bitter brew, as if we were teabags left too long in hot water. But God provides a remedy. In Christ, your heart is scrubbed clean, scoured of brine and bilge. You're made new again! Yes, you'll have to be careful about what you pour into your heart in the future, but you'll never be comfortable with stale and worthless attitudes like those of people who see life as sour, salty, sorrowful. You have more hope than a live dog looking at a dead lion! In Jesus you possess abundant, eternal life— God's gift to you!

Spruce up your faith. Allow your heart to be re-focused by God's rescuing love. Permit it to create the quality of life your Lord expects you to produce. Be guided by an abundant heart!

Chapter 3
The Outcome

Norman Vincent Peale said, "Throw your heart over the fence, and the rest will follow."

I like his advice. Let your heart focus on a project, and all your words, thoughts, commitments and actions will converge into a rich productivity. Likewise, whatever you put into your heart comes out of it again. Your outward deeds and your inward motivations are linked together, and they need careful management if you're to sustain a useful witness for Jesus Christ in the world.

Let's look at an encounter between the Lord and some Pharisees to see how the things in your heart become so important. You'll learn that what your heart concentrates on produces an outcome to match its condition. Directed in a correct manner, your heart achieves much good.

Complaint

The Pharisees complained to Jesus. They traveled from the capital, Jerusalem, where they taught everyone to live by the strict rules of their group. These rigid Pharisees asked Jesus, "Why do your disciples break the tradition of the elders? They don't wash their hands before they eat!" (Mt. 15:2)

The elders' tradition was a large body of oral teaching used to interpret the Old Testament. It wasn't a written tradition; the teachings were passed by word of mouth from teacher to student and memorized. You were drilled in them and discussed them at length until you could recite them instantly. They were firmly planted into the pupil's heart.

The example of the elders' tradition offered to Jesus by the visiting Pharisees was a teaching about washing your hands before meals. The idea wasn't to have clean hands to pick up your food. Germs weren't the concern. The purpose was to have ritually clean hands. You performed a ritual that indicated your desire to be a holy, separated person, someone who lived a strict religious life. It was a matter of dedication and commitment displayed while you took pains to fulfill a prescribed washing ritual.

The Pharisees complained to Jesus that his disciples didn't follow the rigid, time-tested rules of past teachers. This implied that Jesus wasn't teaching his followers the rules. He was tacitly accused of offering slipshod training to his students. Remember: the rules were memorized by people. The Pharisees believed they made the weathered teachings of past rabbis the content of their followers' hearts. They presented folks with good lessons, while Jesus seemed to deliver devious discourses. The Pharisees spotlighted the disciples in order to undercut Jesus. They insulted his status as a bona fide rabbi.

The Pharisees' spirit is alive and well in Christianity today. Members and leaders in some congregations complain whenever tried and true activities of the past aren't done year after year. Whenever new undertakings or methods are suggested, they may complain, "We never did *that* before!" Their hearts are locked into comfortable habits, not into new, growing experiences. They'd rather remain loyal to the spirit of their forbearers in the church than risk a new approach to getting the gospel into more people's souls. When your pastor or other church friend has suggested a new ministry, what was your knee-jerk response? Be careful of trusting the old familiar ways too much. God usually keeps abreast of the best tools for witness and evangelism in each generation. Jesus gave us an example of how the heavenly Father keeps reaching beyond limited human horizons to grander vistas and possibilities. Before you complain about new happenings or practices, look into your heart. What motivates your initial response? Are you in tune with God's Spirit or with a lesser one?

The content of your heart is important. It can lead you astray as it did the Pharisees, or it can lead you into God's new avenues. Deciding whether to follow your heart or to refill it with new goals and skills is crucial to your success as a disciple. Re-focusing what you think and feel is part of staying properly focused. To continue in the centered life, you must frequently reassess the content of your heart. It would have helped the Pharisees to rethink their complaint before they spoke to Christ.

Confrontation

How did Jesus respond to his critics? He confronted the Pharisees. "And why do you break the command of God for the sake of your tradition?" he asked (Mt. 15:4) The Pharisees' tradition was supposed to uphold God's directives, to sharpen a person's obedience to them and to center one's commitment on God alone. Instead, the Pharisees elevated their traditions above scripture, and their vision of God's current activity came unglued. It diverged from God's will instead of converging on it.

Jesus pointed out their mistaken attitude. They noted the command to honor parents, but they tried to find a way around its hard implications. What implications? Well, you honor your parents when they're old by taking care of them. If they need food or clothing, you pay out of *your* pocket. But the Pharisees evaded God's command. So Jesus confronted them, "…you say that if a man says to his father or mother, 'Whatever help you might otherwise have received from me is a gift devoted to God,' he is not to 'honor his father' with it. Thus you nullify the word of God for the sake of your tradition" (Mt. 15:5-6).

The Pharisees nullified, abolished, God's law in order to do what they wanted to do—protect their finances! Jesus pointed out their mistaken attitude by giving them an example of it. Their rules were used to *disobey* the Lord God's commands as easily as to obey them.

Canadian filmmaker David Cronenberg said, "I think of horror films as art, as films of confrontation. Films that make you confront aspects of your own life that are difficult to face."

Jesus exposed the Pharisees to a horror show. He forced them to meet part of their character head-on that they preferred not to notice. The Pharisees were hypocrites, and Jesus told them to their faces. How? He condemned them using Isaiah's words.

> "These people honor me with their lips,
>> but their hearts are far from me.
> They worship me in vain;
>> their teachings are but rules taught by men."
>
> Matthew 15:8-9

Jesus challenged the Pharisees about undercutting God's word. Their beloved scriptures condemned them. Their hearts wandered beyond God. Their mouths spouted false praise. Vanity—uselessness—stained their worship. What a criticism! The Pharisees believed they were the only people in Judaism who were focused on God. Jesus said their hearts were elsewhere. What an insult!

The Lord deepened his offense in their eyes when he warned the surrounding crowd to beware of the mistaken attitude of the Pharisees. As Matthew recorded,

Jesus called the crowd to him and said, "Listen and under-stand. What goes into a man's mouth does not make him 'unclean,' but what comes out of his mouth, that is what makes him 'unclean'" (Mt. 15:10-11).

Jesus warned the crowd not to follow the Pharisees' ritual of washing their hands before meals in order to be ritually clean and acceptable to God. What makes you unacceptable to God isn't what you put into your mouth, but what comes out of it.

Do you hear what Jesus was driving at? He taught the crowd the need to guard their hearts, to know what they contained inside themselves, because the things inside will exit the heart into words and deeds.

If your heart's content is evil, you spout evil from your lips. Isn't this where anger comes from? Isn't it what causes lies, unkindness and hatred to be expressed? From within your soul out into the air, the sound of your words carries to another person's ears the truth about who you are. If you're unclean on the inside, filth flows from the heart, doesn't it? There's no way around it. Whatever you pour into yourself ejects itself into the world. Your heart determines the value of your most sacred relationships with other humans and with God.

A young man pursued his career with difficulty. He had to walk with two crutches because his legs were weak. His colleagues watched him struggle up and down the hallways of their business office. Some admired him, and others avoided him. But the fellow himself was always cheerful. In the lunch room, a co-worker asked why he had his physical problem.

After he answered, "Polio," the colleague asked how he managed to handle his job's demands with his handicap.

The young man answered, "Well, it never got to my heart."

Your heart is important because what you allow into it guides your behavior. This is why Jesus confronted the complaining Pharisees. He wanted them to peer inside themselves and discover why they acted toward him as they did. He believed such a self-inspection would lead them to examine how they behaved toward God. The Pharisees would move to the level of the motivations and commitments that stimulated their lifestyle.

At the root of our characters rests the reasons we act as we do. "Oh, study your hearts!" warned the Puritan preacher John Flavel. "Watch your hearts! Keep your hearts!" Pay attention to your life's principal focus!

Clarification

The disciples asked for clarification of Jesus' meaning. Even they were a little dull-witted about this important matter. As if Jesus didn't know, they asked him in private, "Do you know that the Pharisees were offended when they heard this?" (Mt. 15:12*b*) Jesus explained to his followers how the Pharisees were like plants the heavenly Father didn't put in his garden. They'd be plucked out of it like weeds! Following the Pharisees would be like the blind leading the blind. The disciples would stumble about, just as the Pharisees staggered around.

Jesus could see how his own disciples weren't aware of the intensity of the question about the things people put within their intellects and emotions. We all busily stuff into ourselves the concerns others voice in their words, the ideas inspired by experience, or the feelings created by a tragedy. We pack into ourselves more and more thoughts and emotions all the time. We fill ourselves up and sometimes overflow into zeal for a particular line of thought. Our hearts become impacted, grown inward, too full to absorb a new layer of fearful impressions or angry moods. Then we burst! Rage spurts out! Suspicion of others erupts. Relationships trickle into puddles of memory. Our hearts have swollen beyond their capacity. We've lost our devotion to someone else, our ardent surrender to God, or our sharp-edged loyalty to anyone but ourselves. Our deceptive images of what we want to be are the outcome. We're now hypocrites! We believe we're good, earnest, and dedicated companions on a quest for holiness. Yet we've walked away from genuine faithfulness, because our hearts slid into the mud of sin. Jesus needed to clarify for the disciples how intensely urgent was the content of their hearts.

As Peter so often did, he spoke for all the disciples and requested Jesus to explain more of the meaning behind his confrontation with the Pharisees.

Christ remarked about the disciples' dullness of mind and, in order to enlighten them, he indicated how food passes into and out of the body. "But," he concluded, "…the things that come out of the mouth come from the heart, and these make a man 'unclean.' For out of the heart come evil thoughts, murder, adultery, sexual immorality, theft, false testimony, slander" (Mt. 18-19).

When your heart's content aims at evil, you produce evil with your voice. Jesus named big sins we all hear about in the news media or read about in scintillating novels. Such evils begin inside a person and leap from the heart into the air and into your actions. The outcome of a steady diet of malevolent thoughts and foul emotions ruins you. The filth humanity produces flows from the inside of its soul outward to the world.

This is why managing your heart is crucial to living a good life, to being like Jesus Christ. Robinson Crusoe was right to tell Friday about the devil: "…we pray to God to tread him down under our feet, and enable us to resist his temptations, and quench his fiery darts." Much in today's media isn't worth the money spent to create it. Be cautious of the temptations that spill from television, movies, books, songs, news stories, or the internet. They can misdirect the content of your heart, and what goes into your soul comes out again in the form of words, thoughts and actions.

Charles Spurgeon offered good advice when he told his congregation in London: "You must keep all earthly treasures out of your heart, and let Christ be your treasure, and let him have your heart."

This is also true about the wealth of words and images that pass before your eyes every day. Be sure you allow Christ into your heart so that his Spirit can sort out all the ideas you throw in there with him. Focus on him, and goodness is the outcome of your character.

Commit this thought to memory: *Whatever you put into your heart comes out of it again.*

Chapter 4
The Overflow

The simplest truths are sometimes the hardest to grasp with your mind. They slide easily from your fingers like a slippery fish. Before you realize you've lost them, they're gone out of your hands. This happens with elementary students who struggle to understand the concept behind multiplying numbers. It happens as you try to figure out the moral guidelines of an adult life. Various friends give you conflicting opinions on what's noble and right. Some actions seem good and bad at the same time. How can you make a choice to do purely good deeds all the time? Also, spiritual principles skate smoothly away from you. How can you be certain you follow God's directions? Whether you mull over an intellectual, ethical or spiritual dimension of life, you'll find clear cut matters often the most taxing.

The slippery nature of simple truths explains why Jesus covered the same ground with diverse listeners on several occasions. For instance, he rebuked criticizing Pharisees: "You brood of vipers, how can you who are evil say anything good? For out of the overflow of the heart the mouth speaks" (Mt. 12:34). Then in his Sermon on the Plain, he advised supportive listeners with similar words: "The good man brings good things out of the good stored up in his heart, and the evil man brings evil things out of the evil stored up in his heart. For out of the overflow of his heart his mouth speaks" (Lk. 6:45).

In other words, your life's produce results from who you are on the inside. Your heart's content determines your behavior. To start and end well in your life, fix your gaze properly, not on yourself or the world, but on God and his ways of conduct.

Let's think about this simple truth once again. We need to understand the center of our lives, the core of who we are, because it decides what we do and say, and where we go in life. It determines our root character and our favored ways of expressing it. Our hearts disclose whether our world is good or bad, whether we make people happy or miserable.

Deficient Qualities

A bad person's heart contains a surplus of deficient qualities. As Jesus pointed out, "...the evil man brings evil things out of the evil stored up in his heart." To make his point, Jesus used the word *evil* three times. How can you expect an indecent person to act decently? It seems so obvious that vice begets vice. It's a simple idea. Why is it so difficult to avoid acting in bad ways? Why does wickedness overflow a soul that hoards evil?

You may want to believe that everybody has some goodness buried deeply within him. Stories abound of war heroes who are mean and hard before battle, but who sacrifice themselves quickly to save other soldiers in their unit. Of course, we respect their bravery, and we don't know everything in their hearts at the moment of their sacrifice. A spark of goodness may exist in everyone, but its existence there doesn't change a simple truth: The evil-hearted person makes evil happen around him.

Thieves steal sometimes because they have children to feed, and they can figure no other way to get food for their babies' survival. But a person who has no respect for anybody's property will sooner or later take whatever he wants, either on a whim or deliberately, having planned and rehearsed the crime. A thief's heart tells him it's okay to steal. Some folks may steal out of necessity, but others are thieves because they've delighted to commit their hearts to thievery.

I remember a teenager who broke into a neighbor's home and stole expensive rifles. When caught, he was asked why he took the guns. His answer, "I *wanted* them."

Isn't this why God's commandment declares clearly, "You shall not covet…anything that belongs to your neighbor" (Ex. 20:17)?

Liars also stretch the truth at times because they wish to protect a sensitive person from cruelty. But a person who cares nothing for truth and falsehood will sooner or later tell you a tall tale while she looks you in the eye. And she'll be so good at falsehood that you're duped out of your lifesavings or perhaps just a few hundred dollars.

I've read that researchers have determined that one-fourth of us have told friends or clients lies. Most of our deceptions feel harmless. A woman asks a friend if she looks good in a certain pair of shoes, but her friend considers the shoes hideous. She says, "They look okay to me," because she doesn't wish to offend her friend. Or a doctor might believe his patient does want to hear any bad news and allows some important health details to slip out of sight, merely suggesting a specialist ought to be consulted, "just to be sure." Lying is easy if you're convinced you have someone else's best interest at heart. But the truth is, *you lied*.

Why is bad behavior so easy to accomplish? Because the ground is prepared for seed. Evil people plow their hearts and break up the soil inside themselves with wrong desires. Afterward, theft or a lie or worse behavior suggests itself, then a person develops a plot. Finally, out pops a new thief or a self-deceived liar. After a few heists or deceptions, the sin is habitual, easy. The focal point of bad character is in a person's heart, filled with wrong-headed notions, confused ideas and warped values. What comes out of rancid stew except sickness?

"Growing old," Andri Maurois said, "is no more than a bad habit which a busy man has no time to form." In other words, think yourself old, and you shall act yourself old.

Keep yourself abreast of new deeds to achieve, and you'll be young at heart.

"However mean your life is," Henry David Thoreau offered, "meet it and live it; do not shun it and call it hard names. It is not so bad as you are. It looks poorest when you are richest. The fault-finder will find faults even in Paradise. Love your life." As I understand him, Thoreau wants us to recognize the content of our hearts. If my life seems bad to me, it's because my attitude—*my heart*—is full of mistaken notions.

A bad person's heart contains a surplus of deficient qualities. It's overflow cannot help but to be defective.

Superior Qualities

The opposite is true, too. A good person's heart is filled with a surplus of superior qualities. Jesus said, "The good man brings good things out of the good stored up in his heart…" Again, the Lord emphasized his point by tripling his use of the word *good*. The reason a decent person usually does decent things is that her inner spirit has embraced "whatever is true, whatever is noble, whatever is right, whatever is pure, whatever is lovely, whatever is admirable" (*see* Phil. 4:8). She thinks about such topics. She ponders them long and analyzes how to do them before she sets about practicing them. The stimulus for respectable people is the overflowing goodness packed into their minds and hearts.

William Hazlitt penned this thought: "To be capable of steady friendship or lasting love are the two greatest proofs, not only of goodness of heart, but of strength of mind." Head and heart come together through fondness. Pour in goodness, and goodness flows out.

To make water come up from underground, a pump must be primed. Water has to be trickled down into its mechanism. Then it's able to draw the ground water out of the earth. So it is with the human heart and mind. You must fill your interior life with the virtue you wish it to propel to the surface. Who you are inside spills over to reach those on the outside. If the "water" in your soul is pure, it will refresh those who "drink" it.

You may believe that everybody is capable of doing evil. Push a good father hard enough, and he'll kill to protect his child. Many movies and television shows have explored the psychological effects on a parent whose child was held hostage. The plots involve a good hero being forced to do bad things—to steal diamonds or to rob a bank—in order to save loved ones. We're all easily persuaded that a holy, faithful Christian could become a nasty antagonist. If you subject him to enough negative motivation, he'll shift his focus from Jesus Christ and will do expedient deeds in order to end the bad incentives. During the early church's persecutions, believers betrayed one another to the authorities.

But the truth hasn't changed. Examine any genuinely good individual, and the upright person will do virtuous, first-rate, worthy deeds almost without effort or without thinking about it. Worthy folks do worthy deeds! It's the core focus within their characters. A good person's life is saturated with respectability, morality and nobility so that virtuous deeds come as naturally as breathing.

Superior qualities overflow a good personality. Those who are excellent people at heart take off falsehood and re-clothe themselves with integrity. Unwholesome talk doesn't cross their lips because unwholesome thoughts don't enter their minds or slosh around in their hearts. They're imitators of Christ. As Jesus spoke honestly, they speak frankly, directly, sincerely, without the tiniest tidbit of deception. United with Christ, they're encouraged to comfort others, to act tenderly, and to have compassion even when reviled themselves. A good heart so overflows with superior qualities that it emits only goodness, only kindness, only honor and morality. A superior person is a cut above others because of the material stored at the hub of his personality. The mainstay of his soul is virtue. The crux of his decisions is holiness. He's like Jesus Christ and does every deed with an eye on his exceptional Lord's integrity.

I've known tough people. Their lives were hardened by poverty or crushed by affliction, but they always stood up with grace and acted with integrity. Their words were always kind, filled with praise for others who helped them a little. On the outside, they sometimes appeared to be crusty folks, grave in their thoughts and brusque in manner. But their hearts were good. If you needed it, they'd give you the shirts off their backs. They were honorable folks because the nucleus of their souls was virtuous. Inside, they were blameless, and so the superior quality of their lives seeped through.

A sad truth is that you sometimes live with such a high-class individual and miss the exclusive privilege that is yours. As James Douglas suggested, "Generally the man with a good wife, or the woman with a good husband, or the children with good parents discover too late the goodness they overlooked while it was in full bloom."

Too often a person looks backward on her life to discover how seldom she appreciated her husband. Only after his death or departure does she realize what a charmed life they shared for decades. Her spouse was a better man than some of her friends married. He found work whenever he was laid off. He put food on the table and gave the children his undivided attention. On and on her delayed musings go until it dawns on her than the man was a good one at heart. Why was she so difficult toward him? Too often she missed the overflow of his superior qualities. Now they're mere memories.

She shouldn't dwell morosely upon the chagrin or the sadness of not seeing her spouse's fine character in time to truly enjoy him. Let the widow or the divorcee change herself. She can turn over in her mind what made him a kinder, friendlier person than she realized. She can ask herself how to learn similar virtues, how to re-fill the content of her own heart, the thoughts of her mind. She can become what she was not. The transformation begins inside herself, but its benefits will spread out to touch her children, neighbors and friends. When we neglect the goodness around us, we can redeem the loss by re-examining our souls and seeking God's mercy to begin again. He can fill us to excess with love, joy, peace, compassion, and all things noble or pure or wise.

This maturation starts when the heart is surrendered to God through Jesus Christ. Concentrate on the Lord first, allow his worthiness to form itself within you, and your focus is redirected into excellent behavior, into centered living.

A Quaker bought a mule to plow his fields, though he'd never used a mule before. After he hitched the animal to the plow, he snapped the reins and called for it to move. The mule didn't budge. The Quaker tried again. The mule refused to move. The Quaker felt anger flood his heart. He walked in front of the animal, raised his fist to hit it on the forehead, but he stopped before beating it. He spoke to the stubborn creature: "Mule, thou knowest I cannot strike thee for I am a peaceful Quaker. Thou knowest that I may not curse thee. But thou shouldst also know that I may sell thee to a Presbyterian preacher who will beat thee for me!"

Do you want to prevent your life from unraveling? Then hear what Jesus said: "…out of the overflow of the heart the mouth speaks" (Mt. 12:34). The Lord's teaching is clear and simple. It bears repeating, because we so easily mistake its value. Think about the truth of what he says, and surrender your heart to it. *Your life's produce results from who you are on the inside.*

What behavior is overflowing from within you?

Chapter 5
The Focused Heart

A college freshman ran out of clean clothes. He'd worn everything several times. Finally, he stuffed his duds into a sweatshirt and went to the laundry room. Two girls were there, and he was embarrassed by his filthy clothes. So he shoved the entire ball into a washer, then a dryer. He took the ball to his room to separate the clothing. That's when he discovered how *not* to do laundry. On the outside, the ball was dry, but the clothes at the core were damp, almost wet. And none of them were clean!

The same outcome is brought about when you leave your heart in a balled-up mess to be untangled later. If your interior life is crucial to who you are, what you do and how you speak, isn't it a good idea to keep your heart tuned up and ready for any situation? Unfortunately, many people allow their hearts to be overrun and to fall into disrepair as a result of the hectic days they spend just getting along in life. Their days become burdensome. Their moods shift quickly. They become difficult people. How can we keep our hearts in tiptop shape so that we can handle whatever comes our way?

Let's end our look at the human heart by hearing from the apostle Paul. His ideas in Romans 10 are complex, but we can pull out his comments regarding the Christian hearts. Paul teaches this truth: *With your heart, you believe and are made right with God.* This is how to maintain a strong interior guide, a good heart.

What's the apostle driving at?

The Redeemed Heart

First, he says, A Christian has a redeemed heart. As he wrote, "…if you confess with your mouth, 'Jesus is Lord,' and believe in your heart that God raised him from the dead, you will be saved" (Rom. 10:9). When Christ is in your heart, your lips say so. You cannot help speaking his name, nor can you halt giving a silent witness about him in your behavior. It's also impossible for your attitude to betray doubt about his authority over you. In thought, word and deed, you convey to everybody that Jesus is your Master, because you're focused on him.

A major benefit of confessing Jesus Christ before others comes in receiving the approval of God. With grace, the Father in heaven smiles upon all who receive his Son as their rescuer. Liberation from the most terrible effect of sin, eternal death, is credited to the man or woman who admits the power of the Nazarene over his or her life. Jesus is more than a positive influence on your character development. He does more than get the last word in any decision regarding you. He has a license to do with you as he pleases. His authority over you is complete, and you're willing to acknowledge his power publicly. You tell the people around you, "Jesus is my Lord." God confirms your confession by an internal knowledge that you are saved. You're accepted by the Father into the family.

In a small group Bible study, I recall a lively discussion about the question: "What's the least you can do to be a Christian?" Some said, "You have to believe, and that's it." Others insisted, "No! You have to do what God wants, too." A few answered, "Nothing! You can't do anything. Even faith is God's gift." If the apostle Paul had been among us that evening, I think his answer would have come in these words: "…if you confess with your mouth, 'Jesus is Lord,' and believe in your heart that God raised him from the dead, you will be saved." These two beliefs are what separate Christian people from all other folks.

Believers can differ on all kinds of issues. The worship of Christ occurs in many ways. Christians can draw out various assumptions about what faithful disciples may do, where they can go, and who can be received as close friends. Their music is played in styles old or new, simple or complicated. But two beliefs rest at the core of what makes us Christ's people. You proclaim with your mouth, "Jesus is Lord." That means you verbally identify yourself with him and publicly announce yourself as a disciple. You must let people know where your allegiance lies—with Christ. Still, you must hold a second particular belief deep within your consciousness, the faith that God didn't abandon his Son in a grave. Within your heart, you must believe Jesus was raised from the dead, or you cannot claim the title of Christian. The resurrection is a dividing line between Jesus' disciples and people of the broader world. Those who won't claim Jesus as Lord have trouble believing in his resurrection, too. Why? These are the two distinguishing marks of Christ's followers: an audible confession of Jesus' lordship, plus a deliberate awareness that the resurrection took place.

Paul says, in effect, "If those two truths are in your life, then you can be certain you're among the saved." You have no adequate reason to doubt your deliverance. A Christian has a redeemed heart. This is proven by your confession and your faith, and it's carried out in your day-to-day activities.

Someone may tell you this is arrogance on the part of Christians. Who are we to believe that God has chosen us and not someone else for redemption? Besides, if it's our mere belief that Jesus is Lord and that he was raised from the dead, then there can be no satisfactory proof of what we say. Perhaps so, since your critic will not announce a shred of confidence in Jesus' lordship or put any credence into his resurrection. You and the detractor have come to a blank wall. Neither one can scale it. A hedge separates you and ends further conversation. When one person accepts Jesus' lordship and the other rejects it, fellowship is stripped away by the opposing content in two hearts. If two people disagree over the validity of Jesus rising from the dead, communion between them has ended, and the faith or disbelief within the two hearts is the cause, not any mistakenly perceived arrogance.

With a redeemed heart comes the burden of belonging to one segment of humanity which is now divided from a portion of the human race that fails to see the truths at the core of Christianity. The separation is sad, regrettable, and real.

The Justified Heart

Next, Paul tells us, A Christian has a justified heart. As he wrote, "…it is with your heart that you believe and are justified" (Rom. 10:10*a*).

The center of your life is where you begin to get right with God. Your heart is the place he chooses to begin the mighty labor that leads to your salvation. Being all-wise, God refuses to wave a wand and pronounce anyone who has been belligerent toward him now to be an acceptable person. His grace enters every heart trying to nudge and caress it into admitting the need to be forgiven and restored. God plants the seeds of belief within your heart. He attempts to enliven that faith and bring it into the open, but your heart has to respond to his tapping finger. It has to lean toward him, to incline his direction where the sun may spread out its life. As your heart receives the Gardener's gentle stroke, faith in Christ develops, and the divine Farmer approves. You're made right with God by the faith in your heart. You're justified.

The huge problem that makes God's intervention in human life necessary is sin. Because you and I choose consistently to do what opposes God's definitions of what's good, right and holy, we're subject to the penalty of sinfulness. Our relationships with others are broken or weakened by our sins. Our intimate knowledge of the Lord's emphatic love is distorted into fear, distrust and compromise by our sins. Broken bits and pieces of our identity pile up into a heap of rubble, and few truly wonderful accomplishments come from us when our hearts aren't right with the heavenly Father. Everything we touch is tarnished by transgression. We aren't right with God or other people or the natural world where we must live our days. We need to be justified. We need to be made right with the Lord again. So God intervened in our deplorable situation by coming to us in the person of his beloved Son, Jesus of Nazareth.

Jesus' death on the cross, with the resurrection that followed his burial, removed the cause of our brokenness. He sacrificed himself to remove our sins. His resurrection is God's warranty, a guarantee, that this good news is genuine and trustworthy. So with your heart, you believe and are made right with God. You're justified because of what Jesus did, and because you believe it. You're now on the road to centered living.

The content of your heart reveals the destiny of your soul and body. This is why the human heart is so important to God's activity in the world. Who you are starts at the core of your personality, in your heart. What you believe about the world, about yourself, and about your Creator determines what becomes of you. The heart is the wellspring of life, or the cesspool of death!

"…it is with your heart that you believe and are justified."

The challenge God faces is to reach the center of your life and to convince you that you're loved from on high. Do you believe he cares about you so much that he raised Jesus from the dead for your sake, for your salvation? Then all is well with your life and world! A Christian has a justified heart that has begun focusing in God alone.

The Confessing Heart

Finally, Paul says a Christian has a confessing heart. As he wrote, "…it is with your mouth that you confess and are saved" (Rom. 10:10*b*). Recall what you've learned before: Your mouth speaks the content of your heart. If anger seethes within your soul, you're going to speak profanity or make horrible accusations about someone among your neighbors or in your family. If compassion grips the center of your being, you're going to speak tender words to the afflicted. When your heart is overrun by physical exhaustion, you're going to moan about how poorly you feel and go to bed. When you surrender your heart to the love divine that excels all other loves, your mouth praises and proclaims the wonders of your Savior. "…it is with your mouth that you confess and are saved." It is within your heart and by your confession that God defeats the evil force that battles to control your world.

Friday listen to Robinson Crusoe's explanation of Satan and God struggling in the Christian soul. He voiced a question that bothers many people. Friday asked Crusoe, "…if God much strong, much might as the devil, why God no kill the devil, so make him no more do wicked?"

Truth is, God struggles fiercely in every human heart all day long every day to defeat the hellish energy hiding within all sinful human beings. His strength is exerted in our hearts when we accept the truth that Christ's mission to earth was successful. When you and I admit that Jesus is Lord and that God raised him from the dead, God kills the devil and ruins his power to do wickedness.

Before light bulbs, our homes were often illumined at night by kerosene lanterns. To keep the luminaries bright and useful, the wick had to be trimmed straight across so that it burned evenly. The glass globes on the lamps had to be regularly cleaned of black soot, and kerosene had to fill the small tank at the lantern's bottom.

The Christian heart is much the same. You can trim the wick and wash the globe, that is, you can live a fine life, following good ethical principles. Yet if the tank isn't filled, then nothing happens. Unless your heart is filled with God's grace and the Spirit of God, no light burns in your character.

At the center of your life—within your heart—lies the subject matter of your days and nights on earth. There relax the noble, pure, lovely and admirable truths of who you are. There rest the motives for where you go, what you do, how you speak, and who you're becoming. Be careful of your heart. Consider the layers, coverings and deposits you spread over this foundation. What you build up within your soul becomes your character's strength, or the weakness of your personality.

Remember: You will confess, you will shout abroad to the listening world, the things that lie deep within you. Is Christ your foremost focus? Have you swept clean the debris of hatred or unholiness? Do you fill the chambers of your heart with the life you draw from Jesus the Nazarene? A Christian has a confessing heart, and it tells everybody what is really believed. It reveals the center of your life. It tells the world who you are.

After World War II, British field marshal Montgomery took a seat in Parliament. During a heated discussion, he spoke loudly to the lord next to him, "Excuse me, please, I'm having a coronary thrombosis." As he left the room, people chuckled, thinking he joked regarding the debate. But the doctors at the hospital confirmed that he was, indeed, having a heart attack.

Be careful about your heart. What's going on inside you? Is centered living happening in your soul? Be sure the core of your being is in good shape, aimed at Christ. Why? Because with your heart, you believe and are made right with God or wrong with the world.

BOOK 5
A CROWN FOREVER
AND OTHER SERMONS

Sermon 1
A Crown Forever
1 Corinthians 9:24-27

Why should you bother to live the Christian life? It seems to be easier *not* to follow Jesus Christ's morality, and it seems to be more rewarding financially to follow the world's morality. Why should you bother to live the Christian life?

A variety of reasons offer themselves as motives to obey Christ. His ways make sense, and if everybody followed them, the world would be a wonderful place. That's a good reason to live the Christian life. Another motive is to offer honest, faithful conduct to the Lord as a thank offering for all he's done for you. By living according to his teachings, you show gratitude for your salvation and for his mercy. That's a good reason to live the Christian life.

In 1 Corinthians 9, the apostle Paul offered another motive for following Jesus Christ's way. His message was simple. As an athlete has one goal in mind and disciplines himself to reach it, so *a Christian is self-disciplined for a purpose. His reward is a crown that lasts forever.* Let's look at Paul's motivation for living the Christian life.

An Eternal Prize

The apostle wrote, "Do you not know that in a race all the runners run, but only one gets the prize? Run in such a way as to get the prize. Everyone who competes in the games goes into strict training. They do it to get a crown that will not last; but we do it to get a crown that will last forever" (1 Cor. 9:24-25).

Paul wrote to the church in Corinth, whose members wanted to live the good life as defined by non-Christian people in Corinth. The city's Christians were reluctant to give offerings to help believers in Judea, desiring to keep their money close to home. Some of them enjoyed feasts at pagan temples, while others were critical of the practice. The Corinthian church loved to argue, even to the extent of taking one another to court, and sexual immorality was tolerated within the congregation. It was difficult to tell Corinthian Christians apart from their disbelieving neighbors. What were they doing with their salvation in Jesus Christ? How did their lives honor him? What were they working for?

A better life was offered by Paul. His friends were Christians; they ought to live as Christians. The community around them needed to see a difference in their characters. They were Jesus Christ's people. Their neighbors should be able to point and say, "Now, there's an honest man. There's a generous person. There's a woman who's a credit to the city." Christians in Corinth needed to work for an eternal crown. More than respect and praise from their neighbors, as valuable as that was, they needed to work for God's satisfied approval of their daily deeds. Christians work for an eternal prize.

A young butcher was told he could get all the business of a big hotel if he gave the hotel's food buyer a fifth of whiskey. He decided it was worth a try. The man placed an order. After every bottle of whiskey, an order was placed. Soon the hotel was one of the butcher's biggest customers.

But the butcher was a Christian, and soon he felt uncomfortable about trading whiskey for meat orders. He decided to stop aiding and abetting the other man's bad habits. As a result orders ceased coming from the hotel, but so did business from other customers. The butcher went bankrupt. The butcher's name was James Cash Penney, who later found the J. C. Penney Company, and he never regreted the stand he took on his Christian principles.

Christians work for an eternal prize. Take a hard look at yourself. What are your days like? Does anyone receive kindness from you in a day's time? A phone call, card or personal visit? Does anyone give God thanks for your friendship? Does everyone receive a gentle answer from you, even when they're irritable people to deal with? What fruit is there from your commitment to Jesus Christ? How do people know the Lord owns your heart and soul?

Late in life, Sarasate, the violinist, was hailed as a genius by a critic. "Genius!" Sarasate responded. "I've practiced fourteen hours a day for thirty-seven years. Now they call me a genius!"

Do you work for an eternal prize? Others may not appreciate the way you live up to Jesus Christ's teachings. But what does that matter? You aren't working for their praise of the good things you do. You're working for an eternal prize. You want to hear God say, when you stand before him, "Well, done, good and faithful servant!"

A Desired Prize

The apostle Paul also wrote, "...I do not run like a man running aimlessly; I do not fight like a man beating the air. No, I beat my body and make it my slave so that after I have preached to others, I myself will not be disqualified for the prize" (1 Cor. 9:26-27).

Paul held himself up as an example of how to live the Christian life. He wasn't being boastful or saying he was better than others. Paul tried to motivate the Corinthian believers to put their faith in Jesus Christ to work in productive ways. He suggested self-discipline as a beginning. As a runner trains hard for a race, as a boxer does more than beat the air with his fists, so Christians in Corinth should discipline themselves for the contest. They needed to do the little things first, the easy ones, building up day after day to more difficult chores in holy living. Master one Christian skill, then two, three. In time, like trained athletes, the Corinthians would win the race.

"Religion means work," wrote Henry Ward Beecher. "Religion means work in a dirty world. Religion means peril. The world is to be cleansed by somebody; and you are not the called of God if you are ashamed to scour and scrub."

Christians work for a desired prize. We want God's kingdom to come, and come it will—whether we help it arrive or not. But it would be wonderful when the kingdom is at last here on earth in all its glory to hear a divine voice say, "Thank you, my faithful son. Thank you, my faithful daughter." Christians work for a desired prize—the coming of God's kingdom on earth, and the satisfied gratitude of the Lord.

> Who does God's work will get God's pay,
> However long may seem the day,
> However weary be the way;
> Though powers and princes thunder, "Nay!"
> Who does God's work will get God's pay.
> He does not pay as others pay,
> In gold or land or raiment gay;
> In goods that vanish and decay;
> But God in wisdom knows a way,
> And that is sure—let come what may.
> Who does God's work will get God's pay.
>
> —*Anonymous*

Do you desire the eternal prize? You can live the Christian life for a variety of good reasons. Because you understand that Christ's teachings make sense and will create a better world. Or because you want your life to honor God. Or as an athlete has one goal in mind and disciplines himself to reach it, so you will want to be self-disciplined for a purpose. Work for an eternal prize and desire it with all your heart. You aren't working to earn salvation; instead, you're working to make your salvation count for something in this sin-filled world. Work to get a crown that will last forever.

Amen

Sermon 2
The Crown of Righteousness
2 Timothy 4:1-8

Did you ever try to do something only to have it turn out half-baked? Maybe it was the construction of a piece of furniture or the writing of a song. Maybe you tried to visit in a nursing home and found the wheelchairs and medical equipment made you so nervous you cut your visit short. You left feeling guilty about such a poor visit to an elderly friend. Whatever it was that turned out badly, or of lesser quality than you hoped, did you feel like a failure?

If the attempt was to do a deed of Christian service, and if you failed to be the success you wanted to be, did you feel guilty? Well, stop remorseful! You've been promised a reward just for having tried.

Let's look at the apostle Paul's advice to his friend Timothy, because it'll ease this burden you feel.

A Charge to Keep

Paul gave Timothy a charge to keep. "In the presence of God and of Christ Jesus, who will judge the living and the dead, and in view of his appearing and his kingdom, I give you this charge: Preach the Word; be prepared in season and out of season; correct, rebuke and encourage—with great patience and careful instruction" (2 Tim. 4:1-2). The apostle was in prison at Rome, near the end of his life, and he wanted his co-worker to take up the torch in Jesus Christ's cause. So Paul gave Timothy a charge to keep.

As a young preacher, Timothy was to enter his ministry with his mind clear about the presence of God and Christ with the church, and with himself. He was to remember Jesus as judge of the living and the dead, and sooner or later he'd return. The kingdom of heaven would be established, and Timothy was to give his energy to preaching this gospel. He was to be prepared in all circumstances to serve the Lord Jesus. He was to do a church leader's work, correcting misconceptions about Christ, about God's will, rebuking those who didn't bring their lives into line with the Lord's plan, encouraging those who tried to live up to their commitment. Timothy was to work with patience and care.

Paul warned Timothy about what he could see ahead for the church. "For the time will come," he wrote, "when men will not put up with sound doctrine. Instead, to suit their own desires, they will gather around them a great number of teachers to say what their itching ears want to hear. They will turn their ears away from the truth and turn aside to myths" (2 Tim. 4:3-4). When bad times came, Paul wanted him to keep his head clear, to persevere, doing his evangelistic work and performing his duties well. Paul gave Timothy a charge to keep.

John Henry Jowett was a famous British preacher. One of his church's members talked to a friend and told the friend how he listened to Jowett preach every Sunday. "Wow!" the friend answered. "What a terrible responsibility!"

God gives every Christian a charge to keep. Some are pastors and teachers who must proclaim the truths of the good news; some will be the learners. Others will minister comfort to the afflicted and aid to the poor. Others listen to mourners or give liberally to Christian projects, either their time, talent or treasures. Not everyone will appreciate what we do, but you and I have a charge to keep.

Missionary doctor Albert Schweitzer wrote about the way primitive peoples view responsibility to others. "To the primitive," Schweitzer said, "the idea that he should be concerned for others has narrow limits. His concern is confined, first to his blood relations, then to the members of his tribe, who represent to him the family enlarged."

Schweitzer explained how, if he asked a patient in his hospital to do something for a bedfast patient, the person would do it, but only if the patient in bed was from his tribe. About all others, he'd tell Schweitzer, "He is not my brother."

Do you understand the charge God gives you? You aren't asked to help yourself, but to help others—and all others are your kin. You may be expected by God to teach people about Jesus Christ, to feed, clothe or shelter others, to console, counsel or encourage. In different contexts, you have different charges to keep. You may be called to teach your children or grandchildren about God's love in Christ. You may be called to serve as a church officer or do crafts for a fundraiser to support Christ's work. Whatever the charge, you're to fulfill it with patience and care. Do you understand the Lord's charge to you? How do you try to live up to it?

A Charge Well-Kept

Paul believed he kept his charge well. As he told Timothy, "...I am already being poured out like a drink offering, and the time has come for my departure. I have fought the good fight, I have finished the race, I have kept the faith. Now there is in store for me the crown of righteousness, which the Lord, the righteous Judge, will award me on that day—and not only to me, but also to all who have longed for his appearing" (2 Tim. 4:6-8). Like a good athlete, the apostle finished his contest. He was convinced he'd kept the Lord's charge to him.

Having completed the work God assigned, Paul prepared to leave this world. In prison at Rome, he knew execution was near. When he died, he'd be rewarded by Jesus Christ for his labor. A crown of righteousness was set back for him, waiting his Lord's arrival. And it wasn't only for him that such crowns were laid aside. Paul believed any Christian who serves the Lord Jesus well has a crown of righteousness stored up for him and will receive it when our righteous judge returns.

What is a crown of righteousness? Paul used a word which can be translated as "crown," but it isn't the golden crown of a king. It's the crown of laurel leaves given to an athlete who wins a race or a wrestling match. The reference to righteousness is to your good, useful life which is poured out as a service to Christ. Your efforts for the kingdom won't go unnoticed. God plans to reward the useful things you do in his Son's name.

"When great causes are on the move," said Winston Churchill, "we learn that we are spirits, not animals, and that something is going on in space and time, and beyond space and time, which, whether we like it or not, spells duty."

Christianity is a great cause—the greatest ever—and it's on the move. Have you tested the depth of your soul, the height of your commitment? God is rescuing the world from sin and death, and he's assigned you a part in the great work. It's your duty to accomplish this work to the best of your ability.

Any Christian can keep his charge well. It doesn't require anything you think may be lacking in your training or your devotion. To keep your charge well simply requires that you do something godly, something Christlike, each day. A kind word to a harried person, or a well-worded rebuke of a sinful person. A touch on a sick brow or a tough reminder of a person's higher duty. Everyday, if you're looking for it, Jesus Christ brings someone across your path or into your mind whom you're asked to serve. Perhaps it'll be an obligation in the church. Or it could be outside the church's walls. Whatever it is, are you trying to do it?

While Mother put little Sandra to bed, she noticed all the books, crayons, dolls and toys scattered again across the floor. "Sandra," Mother scolded, "you know you aren't supposed to leave your things scattered around."

Sandra answered, "Mother, I try to keep them picked up. Doesn't it count that I tried?"

How well are you keeping the charge God gives you? It doesn't matter that you succeed in a glorious manner. It matters only that you faithfully try. Are you keeping the charge God gives you? Those who do receive a crown of righteousness.

Amen

Sermon 3
The Crown of Life
James 1:2-12

You receive the crown of life as a reward for perseverance. Many people snicker at this Christian belief, thinking it promises a vain hope to those in bad circumstances. Since you're a believer, this hope is your source of inspiration and determination. It makes you want to forge ahead when times are tough. You know it's true! *You receive the crown of life as a reward for perseverance.*

As the Letter of James says, "Blessed is the man who perseveres under trial, because when he has stood the test, he will receive the crown of life that God has promised to those who love him" (Jas. 1:12). Let's explore this thought further and see how true it is.

The Complete Life

First, how are you blessed by enduring trials? James explained in these words: "Consider it pure joy, my brothers, whenever you face trials of many kinds, because you know that the testing of your faith develops perseverance. Perseverance must finish its work so that you may be mature and complete, not lacking anything" (Jas. 1:2-4).

Perseverance brings you maturity. The best authors bump against the literary equivalent of hard rocks along the shoreline. The best artists feel the pain of separation and loss while engaged in artistic pursuits. The best composers struggle to keep their hearing and continue to compose great music when sounds begin to disappear. The best people you know suffer one set-back after another yet never lose their smiles. The best Christians mature in Jesus Christ's kind of life when they face anger, suspicion, ridicule, or betrayal with faith. They know God carries the burden with them, and so they mature in the Christian graces.

How are you blessed by enduring trials? James explained further: "If any of you lacks wisdom, he should ask God, who gives generously to all without finding fault, and it will be given to him. But when he asks, he must believe and not doubt, because he who doubts is like a wave of the sea, blown and tossed by the wind. That man should not think he will receive anything from the Lord; he is a double-minded man, unstable in all his ways" (Jas. 1:5-8).

Perseverance brings you maturity. You learn where lies the source of your most dependable help: *in the Lord God, who loves you.* When problems baffle you, the Lord has wisdom to share with you, and you turn to him quickly for the insight. From scripture and in prayer, you gain what the world lacks—guidance from above. God doesn't blame you for the initial failure to understand a problem; he offers good advice. But you have to ask for it with confidence, not vacillating between wanting to know his will and wanting to do it your way. Those who receive the Lord's wisdom are those who are determined to get it. As you grow in your determination to know and follow God's counsel, you gain maturity. Perseverance brings you growth in grace.

About perseverance, Henry David Thoreau wrote, "I know of no more encouraging fact than the unquestionable ability of man to elevate his life by a conscious endeavor." Anyone who works at having a better life than he currently has will probably get it, not always in monetary terms, but in terms of human growth, strength of heart, and nobility of character. For Christians who seek God's help to face daily trials, the growth is a development of the soul. Perseverance brings you maturity.

The Circumstances of Life

Next, how is your faith proven to be genuine? James explained in these words: "Blessed is the man who perseveres under trial, because when he has stood the test, he will receive the crown of life that God has promised to those who love him" (Jas. 1:12).

Perseverance carries you through the test. It proves the genuine nature of your faith. In the crucible of suffering, your belief in Jesus Christ's good will toward you is tempered. A steel-hardened buttress is added to your character by times when you endure difficulty with patience, courage, and reliance on God. The Holy Spirit works in your heart and mind to turn doubts aside, to make faith a little firmer, to enliven your knowledge that you have a divine Friend who stays closer than a brother. While your faith in Christ allows God to help in your daily struggles, you find that you make it through crisis and irritation, not unscathed, but not mortally wounded either. Perseverance carries you through the test. Both you and God now know how strong your faith has become. "Perseverance," wrote Plutarch, "is more prevailing than violence; and many things which cannot be overcome when they are taken together, yield themselves up when taken little by little" (*Life of Sertorius*). Rather than return anger for anger or accusation for accusation, learn to endure, because a piece at time the trouble is overcome, and you become a strong person whose power is build on faith in Christ. The circumstances of your life will become better.

James explained another testing of a person's faith. "The brother in humble circumstances," he wrote, "ought to take pride in his high position. But the one who is rich should take pride in his low position, because he will pass away like a wild flower" (Jas. 1:9-10).

A hot desert wind called the sirocco blows out of the Palestinian wilderness and dries up the few green plants which grow in the harsh climate. Blossoms are destroyed, and plants lose their beauty. Riches fade just as easily, said

James, and the person who depends on them treads unstable ground. Christians who are rich must learn to take pride in their status as Jesus Christ's disciples rather than pride in their wealth and possessions. Christians in humble circumstances, who are neither rich nor destitute, have to learn the value of being without worldly goods. Christ must come first for both the rich and the nearly poor. Only he makes a distinction worth having. Find him, rely on him, whether you're rich or not. This is a test of your faith. Trust Christ above all else, because perseverance carries you through this trial of your faith.

The Crown of Life

Now, how do you receive the crown of life? James explained in his letter: "Blessed is the man who perseveres under trial, because when he has stood the test, he will receive the crown of life that God has promised to those who love him" (Jas. 1:12).

Perseverance rewards you as God promised. He pledged himself to give you a crown of life if you love him. You will love him more than you think possible when you face resentment or anger, abuse and ridicule, with faith that makes Christ your source of strength to carry on. As life batters you down and you stand up again with a hand on the Lord's shoulder, affection for him intensifies in your heart. Your conscious mind is filled with thoughts of how good he is. As your love of God expands, life holds new meaning, new purpose, new vigor. The key to unlocking a wonderful life is to love the Lord, and the key to loving the Lord is to face daily troubles with him at your side. Perseverance rewards you with the crown of life.

As he compared Christianity with other religions in the world, Albert Schweitzer wrote, "The Indian idea of the divine is that it is pure, spiritual essence. It is the ocean into which man, tired of swimming, wishes to sink. The God of the Gospel of Jesus is living, ethical Will, desiring to give to my will a new direction. He says to me: 'Strike out courageously! Do not ask where your efforts will take you on the infinite ocean. It is my will that you should swim'" (*Christianity and the Religions of the World*).

Face up to the testing of your faith, because God wants to reward your perseverance with the crown of life.

Amen

Sermon 4
The Crown of Glory
1 Peter 5:1-4

Are you a church officer? Have you been one in the past? Are you a Sunday School teacher? A group leader? You are, at least, a person of influence with someone. Perhaps you're a parent, neighbor, or co-worker. Then the apostle Peter's words, written thousands of years ago to friends who lived in the area we know as modern Turkey, will be helpful to you. Let's learn from Peter how to serve Jesus Christ better.

Peter's Character

Peter was an elder among other elders. He wrote, "To the elders among you, I appeal as a fellow elder..." (1 Pt. 5:1). Peter wanted church officials to think carefully about his words. He appealed to them as a colleague. He and they together served Jesus Christ as church officers. Peter was an elder among other elders. He'd learned a valuable lesson: *Christ's people have to work together.* Other disciples had to learn this lesson, too. Remember James and John, the thundering sons of Zebedee who conned their mother into asking Jesus for places of honor in the kingdom? They learned through embarrassment to work together with other disciples. Neither of them was greater than the Lord's other followers. Each had a place, and each had work to do.

Are you an elder or church leader? Then you're one among other leaders. You have to work with them, not for yourself or for your own prestige. You must serve side by side with all the Lord's servants in a sacred place, the church.

Cultivate the attitude that you are one among many who serve the Lord.

Peter was also an observer and participant of Christ's sufferings. He wrote, "To the elders among you, I appeal as a fellow elder, a witness of Christ's sufferings..." Having heard the Lord speak of his coming death, having opposed Jesus' suffering and been rebuked for his opposition, having followed Jesus to the high priest's home and watched his trial, Peter understood the affliction and pain Jesus endured for his people. He knew Jesus had compassion for us and was familiar with our human troubles and pains.

In his book *The Joy of Being Human*, Eugene Kennedy wrote, "Perhaps no man ever had more reason for self-pity than the famous 'elephant man' of last century London. Hideously deformed, rejected by a society in which he could not appear except wearing a shawl-like covering that obscured his figures completely, he was befriended by a physician who began the simplest of treatments—he looked on him as a human being, making it possible for him to live in the country and to engage in a limited but varied social life." The doctor witnessed the elephant man's sufferings, and his compassion prompted him to help. The apostle Peter observed Christ's sufferings, and after much personal struggle, he began to tell others what Jesus' pain produced for those who have faith.

Do you understand what Jesus Christ suffered for you? Then you're a witness who must share what you understand with your children, co-workers, neighbors, and any other people you might influence.

Peter was also to share in the glory to be revealed. He wrote to his friends and identified himself as "one who...will share in the glory to be revealed" (1 Pt. 5:1). He was referring to the reward held in store for anyone who serves the Lord faithfully. When Christ comes again, the reward will be given. As Peter and other church leaders had shared the church's work, they'd share the church's reward, too.

As you fulfill your servanthood, remember and don't forget: *A crown of glory waits for you.*

Church Leaders' Character

Peter reminded the elders of their own characters and duty. "Be shepherds of God's flock that is under your care, serving as overseers—not because you must, but because you are willing, as God wants you to be; not greedy for money, but eager to serve; not lording it over those entrusted to you, but being examples to the flock" (1 Pt. 5:2-3). Church leaders were to care for God's people.

Are you a church leader? An officer? A teacher? A leader of women? A youth worker? Then it's your responsibility to care for God's people. As a Sunday School teacher, you have children or adults in a small number to look out for. Do you pray for them? Do you send them birthday greetings? As a group leader, do you care more about getting a task or project finished more than you care what happens to the people in the group? You're responsible for part of God's flock. What kind of shepherd are you?

Church leaders were to practice virtue. So taught Peter. Church leaders are to serve because they're willing. They're to be eager to serve without looking for personal gain. They're to serve by example rather than by a domineering authority. Virtue is the hallmark of faithful church leaders. They act with compassion. They feel the desperation their group members feel when children are foolish, when illness strikes a spouse. They rejoice when God answers prayer. They encourage, chastise, or counsel with integrity. Their virtuous character is known to all.

Are you a church leader? A deacon? A treasurer? Then practice virtue. If you're responsible for church money, you're to be neither too frugal nor to free with it. Let honesty coupled with wisdom be your guide in helping the church spend its resources for God's glory. If you're a deacon, you're responsible to lead the church into works of service, caring for the poor and afflicted. You could act out of motives which boost your ego: "Hey, look at what's been done for unfortunate people!" Or you could provide for the downtrodden out of a motive of genuine concern that they receive both help and guidance toward a better life. One attitude leads to virtue, and the other doesn't. Which is yours?

Church leaders were to avoid wrongdoing. Peter told his friends to lay aside the feeling of obligation: Serve "not because you must, but because you are willing." He told them to lay aside greed and serve with eagerness. He told them to lay aside haughty, lordly attitudes in favor of being examples of humility. Church leaders must be as active in avoiding wrongdoing as they are in pursuing virtue.

Are you a committee member? A committee secretary? Then you're called to avoid every wrongdoing. The manner in which you work on a committee shows whether or not you want to avoid bad conduct. Examine the things you support in committee meetings, as well as the things you oppose. Do the causes you champion reveal the goodness of your character? You're called to avoid wrongdoing.

Preacher Oscar Johnson grew up in east Tennessee, and his father gave him the chore of putting firewood in the wood box. Johnson recalled an evening when he forgot to bring in wood. Before going to bed, he and his father went out to cut wood in the dark. On the last trip to the house, Johnson tried to carry as much as he could in order to avoid one more trip. As his father walked behind him, Johnson struggled with the wood. His father picked him up, firewood and all, and carried him to the wood box, then instructed: "Drop that load in there."

Johnson let go of the wood but held on to the lesson. As his father carried him and told him to drop the wood in the box, so Jesus Christ cares about us, carries us and our sins, and he tells us, "Drop that load in there."

As a church leader, that's your basic job, too. So remember and don't forget: *A crown of glory waits for you because you take care of God's people.*

Jesus Christ's Character

Jesus is the Chief Shepherd. Peter wrote, "...when the Chief Shepherd appears, you will receive the crown of glory that will never fade away" (1 Pt. 5:4). Jesus is the primary Leader, and his people have to follow him. No one else knows what to do all the time. He will reward those who struggle along behind him.

As you lead God's people down any path, do you remind yourself regularly that Jesus Christ is the Chief Shepherd of your life? Develop a daily awareness that the one who guides your steps and protects you along the road is Jesus Christ. Your reward will begin in this life, but it won't be completed now. Jesus is returning, coming again. He left this world to prepare a place for us, and he pledged himself to return for us. As you lead God's people on any journey, do you remind yourself that he is coming again?

Jesus has a crown of glory for his people. He promised to return for us so that where he is we will also be. With him for eternity, we will be rewarded for service rendered well.

A man spoke to his pastor, "You say alot about the glory waiting for Christ's people. I've never found it. Why not?"

"I'll tell you how to find the glory waiting for Christ's servants," the pastor said. "Go to a shoe store and buy a pair of slippers. Go to a grocery store and buy a bag of food. Take what you buy to this address. Also take your Bible along. When you get there, give the slippers and food to the woman who answers the door. Go in and read a psalm to her. Then come back and tell me what happened."

The man was puzzled, but he did as the pastor suggested. The woman who answered the apartment door was old, dressed in rags, with nothing on her feet. The man entered her one-room apartment. He gave her the food, and she smiled. He gave her the slippers, and she said, "Thank you!" He read a psalm to her, and she cried, saying, "Thank you, sir, because I cannot see to read anymore, and the Bible means so much to me."

On returning to the pastor, the man reported, "Reverend, I've found the glory you talk about."

As you fulfill your servanthood, remember and don't forget: *A crown of glory waits for you because you take care of God's people.*

Amen

Sermon 5
Your Crown
Revelation 3:7-13

Opportunity knocks on your door, but soon it's gone. Another opportunity knocks and leaves. Though you sometimes open the door to a new opportunity, often you don't hear it knocking or you aren't ready to entertain it. Perhaps it's an opportunity you don't wish to see, and you let it pass down the street to visit someone else. Yet sometimes you open the door.

Are you satisfied with an opportunity you've acknowledged? Or do you wish a different one would present itself? Human beings, as curious and eager creatures. They always look for new things to do or different places to go or other people to know. They look for new opportunities all the time.

What do you seek? What sort of opportunity appeals to you at this stage in your life?

Commissioned

Jesus Christ presents his people with new opportunities all the time. Through his apostle John, he sent a letter to the church in the ancient city of Philadelphia. Jesus told the church, "These are the words of him who is holy and true, who holds the key of David. What he opens no one can shut, and what he shuts no one can open. I know your deeds. See, I have placed before you an open door that no one can shut. I know that you have little strength, yet you have kept my word and have not denied my name" (Rev.

3:7-8). With these words, the church at Philadelphia was commissioned for a new opportunity.

We aren't told what the opportunity was, but we're told who presented it to the church. One who's holy and true. Jesus is described by two important attributes: he's holy and true, set apart from ordinary givers of opportunity and trustworthy as a giver of opportunity. He's also called the one who holds the key of David, which refers to the key to King David's palace. Jesus is the one who holds the key which unlocks the kingdom of heaven. If he opens the door, it stays open. If he shuts and locks it, the door to the kingdom stays barred. All of this was said to the church at Philadelphia in order to highlight Christ's authority. He rules the church, and when he presents an opportunity for service, no one can remove it. Jesus Christ is the Lord.

Through the apostle John, the Lord presented the church at Philadelphia with an open door. The Christians there could enter God's kingdom, as well as a special service for him, because Jesus provided both the way and means. Some commentators suggest that the location of ancient Philadelphia at the head of a broad plain which led to many cities farther east in Asia Minor was the open door to which Jesus referred. He had situated the church at a strategic place for active missionary work. Perhaps that was their church's unique opportunity. In any event, Jesus said nobody could take their opportunity away. It was theirs alone to seize and to fulfill.

Jesus also pointed out his knowledge of the church's lack of resources. It had "little strength," but Christ was confident of the church, because it hadn't denied his name. He knew they could do the good thing he lay before them. They only had to *want* to do it and success would be theirs. The church was commissioned for a new challenge.

You are commissioned for a new opportunity. I can't tell you what it is, but I can tell you that our Lord presents new opportunities every day. You meet someone you don't know.

Here's a chance to become a friend, and in time to introduce your friend to the Lord, if she doesn't know him already.

Maybe you have more time on your hands these days. Would you volunteer to work at an Indian school run by the Presbyterian Church in New Mexico? An elder from Cadiz, Ohio and his wife retired and plan such an activity for a year, because they saw the Lord present them with an opportunity, and they seized it. You, too, are commissioned every day with a new opportunity to serve the Lord Jesus Christ.

John Ruskin advised, "It is a good and safe rule to sojourn in every place as if you meant to spend your life there, never omitting an opportunity of doing a kindness, or speaking a true word, or making a friend."

Opportunities abound for you. What holds you back from seizing a few of them? What difficulties do you see in your way?

Conserved

Jesus Christ understands the difficulties his people face. He instructed John to write to the church in Philadelphia: "I will make those who are of the synagogue of Satan, who claim to be Jews though they are not, but are liars—I will make them come and fall down at your feet and acknowledge that I have loved you. Since you have kept my command to endure patiently, I will also keep you from the hour of trial that is going to come upon the whole world to test those who live on the earth" (Rev. 3:9-10). The church in ancient Philadelphia was conserved when it met opposition. Christ promised to protect it as it endured difficulty.

Through the apostle John, Jesus pointed out his knowledge of the church's opponents. Some people in ancient Philadelphia wanted Christians to live like Jews, but they were mistaken in the difficulties they raised for the church, or within the congregation. They tried to create doubt about Christ's love for the church's faithful members.

The Lord planned to change the tune of those who opposed his will for the Philadelphia congregation. He was also pleased with those who endured patiently, who tried to fulfill the opportunity he'd given the church. He promised to preserve faithful believers when tough times came upon the whole earth. Jesus understood their difficulties, and he promised to conserve the church as it encountered opposition.

You are also conserved, protected, when you meet opposition. As you face up to the struggles of being a Christian and living in a Christian manner, the Lord strengthens you. He prepares to discipline those who oppose the work you do for his honor. He pledges himself to protect you as you faithfully seize the opportunities he presents. Don't become discouraged. The Lord trusts you, or he wouldn't give you the chance to serve him as he does. Trust him in return, and you'll be helped each step of the journey.

Both the British and foul winter weather were hardships for George Washington's army at Valley Forge, and a lack of food, clothing and morale threatened to undo the Revolution. To boost his men's determination, Washington called for an inspection. As he stood before poorly dressed, hostile troops from New England, the General raised his voice and with a satisfied tone announced, "I have great confidence in the men of Connecticut!" Pride and determination grew visibly in each man.

Through confidence and commitment, Washington and his army made it through the difficult winter. Jesus has confidence in you and presents new opportunities to you all the time. Despite opposition, you're called to endure.

Crowned

Jesus Christ plans to reward his people when they endure trouble for his sake. Through the apostle John, he revealed his plan to the church at Philadelphia. "I am coming soon," he said. "Hold on to what you have, so that no one will take your crown. Him who overcomes I will make a pillar in the temple of my God. Never again will he leave it. I will write on him the name of my God and the name of the city of my God, the new Jerusalem, which is coming down out of heaven from my God; and I will also write on him my new name" (Rev. 3:11-12). The church at ancient Philadelphia was to be crowned, rewarded, when it overcame its difficulties.

Ralph Waldo Emerson expressed the feeling of many people when he wrote, "The reward of a thing done well is to have done it well." As true as it is that satisfaction comes from having done your best when an opportunity presented itself, it's also good to be rewarded in other ways for your efforts, isn't it? Especially good if you've overcome many difficulties.

In Christ's kingdom, you'll be crowned when you overcome difficulty. Jesus' final words to the church at Philadelphia were written to all Christian folks. He said, "He who has an ear, let him hear what the Spirit says to the churches" (Rev. 3:13). What he promised the Christians of the ancient city, he promises to you. Because you faithfully seize the opportunities he presents, you'll become part of the temple which Christ builds, you'll have God's protecting name placed on you, and you'll be sealed with Christ's new name. In other words, no one will steal away your crown. You'll be rewarded for faithful service, and the reward will be more than a feeling of satisfaction at having done a good job for the Lord's honor.

Don't forget. All the time, Jesus Christ gives you a new opportunity, and though you may meet opposition as you try to make the most of it, you'll be rewarded for enduring. Consider this truth carefully: *You must endure to receive your crown.*

Amen

ABOUT THE AUTHOR

Larry L. Armstrong is a retired Presbyterian minister who served churches in Massachusetts, Ohio, and Pennsylvania. He was educated at Grove City College in Pennsylvania and Gordon-Conwell Theological Seminary in Massachusetts. He is the founder of FaithProbe Publications and carries on an active writing and speaking ministry.

In 2005, Larry received a liver transplant to replace his original liver which was destroyed by a congenital condition. Since then, he served as pastor of the First Presbyterian Church of Jeannette, PA until his retirement in July 2011.

Other FaithProbe books by Larry Armstrong include *Patience: Harvesting the Spirit's Fruit* and the forthcoming *In the Shadow with Jesus: A Look at the High Priestly Prayer in John 17.*

About his writing, Armstrong says, "I love to write, because it stretches my awareness of who I am. When I wrote sermons every week, I learned and grew more than my congregations. Now that I'm writing books, I find that the self-examination continues."

Regarding his transplant, he explains that God revealed his grace and kindness in many ways, and through many people. "From church members to doctors and hospital staff, I sensed the Lord's presence as I looked for healing in one of three ways—a miracle, a transplant, or in a way my wife wouldn't let me speak." His faith in Christ's goodness carried him through that time.

He and his wife Elizabeth are the parents of four adult children, who live around the country. They also have a very energetic dog named Finnegan, who is a "whatzit hound." They and the dog make their home in Latrobe, PA and at a cottage north of Pittsburgh.